To —

Thanks ..,
example, & all you do for our
church.

God bless,
Bob Gorton
9/27/09

# Christian Tigers

## Lessons Learned and Timeless Tips From One Who Tried To Be One

Bob Gortner

authorHOUSE®

*AuthorHouse™*
*1663 Liberty Drive*
*Bloomington, IN 47403*
*www.authorhouse.com*
*Phone: 1-800-839-8640*

*First published by AuthorHouse 6/29/2009*

*ISBN: 978-1-4389-7950-2 (e)*
*ISBN: 978-1-4389-7948-9 (sc)*
*ISBN: 978-1-4389-7949-6 (hc)*

*Library of Congress Control Number: 2009904605*

*Printed in the United States of America*
*Bloomington, Indiana*

*This book is printed on acid-free paper.*

# Table of Contents

# Purpose:

We live in a society where competitive advantage and winning seem to be of paramount importance. Unfortunately, how we get there doesn't seem to matter as much as it should. Sports fans will remember quotations from two famous and successful coaches:

"If winning isn't everything, why do they keep score?" ... Vince Lombardi, of the Green Bay Packers

"Nice guys finish last" ... Leo Durocher, of the Brooklyn Dodgers

Scandals continue to abound in the worlds of business, politics, and even the professions--mostly prompted by greed and/or pressure to attain ambitious goals and "win" or rank highly.

Back in the late 1970s, while employed in management with a prestigious and highly ethical management consulting firm, I became increasingly aware of these flaws in our societal fabric. Simultaneously, I observed significant shortcomings in the business and accounting academic programs offered by many of the Christian colleges with which I was familiar. Bright, ethical young people from good families attended these institutions and were taught to deepen their faith and be nice, but were not being adequately equipped with "tools of the trade" necessary to gain employment, contribute, and compete effectively in the tough world of business. These students had the potential to make a difference for good, but were not being taught how to gain respect for their abilities and achievements which would earn them the right to be heard and make a positive impact.

Something definitely appeared to be wrong here--a business world badly in need of ethical improvement while, at the same time, Christian colleges were failing to provide many of their graduates with the training and motivation to help change things for the better. Consequently, I shared these concerns with, and sought advice from, the leaders of the Christian College Consortium, and wound up changing careers and joining a moderately sized Christian liberal arts college in the midwest. Here, I served fifteen years as associate dean and chairperson of the Business, Accounting, and Economics Department; and taught the complete spectrum of management courses.

Together with the BAE faculty, we forged and adopted a vision/ mission of developing our students into "Christian Tigers". Back in New York City, from whence I moved, a young, successful person was often called a "tigah". However, these "tigahs" were often ruthless; and achieved success via deceit, lying, back stabbing, taking unfair advantage of situations, and other forms of unethical behavior. Therefore,some folks thought the term, "Christian Tiger" was an oxymoron, but this is not so. Christian Tigers achieve success by being <u>competent</u> and <u>competitive</u> along with being <u>caring</u> and <u>Christian</u>.

The Christian Tiger concept took root, and we did succeed in creating a highly respected set of programs (majors) through the efforts of an expanded, dedicated, skillful faculty: experiential learning (laboratory courses and internships); involvement of the business community (field trips and guest lecturers); and rigorous courses with elevated expectations. Surveys of alumni and their employers confirmed our faculty's belief that we were on the right track.

Now, in retirement, I continue to encourage the development of Christian Tigers, but my role is, of necessity, different. I have time to ponder my life; which has embraced many trials, temptations, and triumphs; and to describe, in this book, many of my learning experiences and other timeless tips which could/should be helpful to high school seniors, college students, and young professionals--and also to a more mature audience of parents and employers who want to help in the development of these much needed Christian Tigers. This is the purpose of this book.

Readers should find the book to be easy reading, albeit meaningful--mostly anecdotal rather than theoretical. However, each real life experience or close observation described herein contains a practical message which is applicable to young professionals; regardless of their background--religious, racial, or ethnic. If readers ingest and apply just a few of these experiential teachings, I will consider my efforts to be a success.

# Author's Credentials:

This book is not an autobiography. Indeed, I cannot boast of a widely recognized, highly successful, lifetime career such as those of top level leaders like Colin Powell, Jack Welch, Lee Iacocca, and Donald Trump--each of whom have been the subjects of best selling biographies. However, to justify your time spent in reading this book, it is appropriate that I briefly describe my background and career, hoping that many of you will be able to identify personally with what I am attempting to convey, and see applicability to your own situations--past, present and future.

I am a preacher's kid, born in 1930 at the height of a very severe economic depression. Therefore, I learned and lived with frugality--a trait I have practiced throughout my life, sometimes to the dismay of my family. My Dad was a great pastor who worked 70 to 80 hours per week caring for his flock which grew from less than 100 to close to 1,000 during his 30 years of ministry in one suburban town. He survived three heart attacks but succumbed to the fourth at age 65. His tombstone epitaph reads: "Greater love hath no man than this, that he lay down his life for his friends". I learned much about service and brotherly love from Dad, but he didn't provide much guidance in the many secular matters I found myself dealing with as I matured.

Growing up in suburbia, I attended a good public high school and graduated with honors from its college preparatory/scientific program. As elective courses, I was able to take drafting, wood shop, and metal shop--practical subjects which have been helpful throughout my life. I wish such were more widely available today. I played varsity baseball (shortstop and second base) and was selected for the county all-star team in my senior year. I was both a class and student council officer and active in many extra-curricular activities.

I managed to avoid our church's youth group because it appeared to me to be largely populated by "losers" while I wanted to associate with the more popular, "elite" group of kids. I learned, later in life from a very successful pastor, that one way to build a thriving church youth group is to recruit two or more of the most popular Christian kids in the school and encourage them to draw a following. This really does work!

I also was guilty of sneering at the lifetime sports of golf and tennis, considering them to be good for sissies, and not really manly. How wrong I was. Now, I thoroughly enjoy tennis and wish I was better at golf. More about that later.

Working at a neighborhood gas station consumed much of my time during weekends and vacations. Back then, we did a lot more than just pump gas. We changed and fixed tires, put snow chains on and took them off, changed oil and filters and did extensive lubrication work, washed and polished cars, serviced radiators with anti-freeze, and performed minor repairs. I learned, early on, to write up large work orders--often talking customers into having things done which were not really needed. This was my first taste of unethical business practices. At that time, I didn't realize how wrong this was to sell unneeded services. Later in life, I observed a major, nation-wide automotive servicing organization get caught with a practice of paying service managers bonuses based on the magnitude of the work orders they wrote up regardless of whether some of the tasks were needed or not. Much unfavorable publicity followed disclosure of this unethical practice. On balance, however, my work experience during high school years was very beneficial, teaching me how to deal with a wide variety of people, and causing me to learn the value of money and how to budget.

Upon graduation from high school in 1947, shortly after the end of World War II, I was lucky to be accepted by Drexel Institute of Technology, a highly respected engineering school which was flooded by applicants who had served in the war and were deservedly rewarded with G.I.Bill educational benefits. I chose Drexel not only because of its excellent reputation, but also because it offered a mandatory cooperative education program (requiring two years of paid employment, interspersed with my academic work and related to my studies, as a condition for graduation). This compensation, coupled with a half tuition scholarship and living at home, enabled me to pay my way through college with no parental assistance. I majored in Industrial Engineering and enjoyed four outstanding six month co-op work assignments--three of them with a division of Westinghouse which was designing aircraft jet engines, and a fourth period with a division of the Frankford Arsenal which manufactured optical elements for military purposes.

Despite the disadvantages of being a commuting student, as most Drexel students were at that time, I was quite active in extra-curricular endeavors and became a member of Lambda Chi Alpha, a social fraternity which provided opportunity to assume leadership roles and participate in inter-fraternity sports and social events. Alcohol consumption was tightly controlled, and drug usage was essentially non-existent in those days. My performance was rewarded by selection to Who's Who and Phi Kappa Phi, a prestigious, national honors fraternity.

I met a pretty Drexel co-ed early in my freshman year and dated her throughout all of my college years. As graduation approached in 1952, our country was at war with North Korea and I knew that I would be required to serve in the armed services. Consequently, Aileen and I were married four months before graduation, much to the dismay of my mother who thought I was too young to enter a lifetime commitment. We lived happily in a loft apartment during those four months, and I accepted an offer of employment which I never got to experience because I received orders to report to Naval Officers' Candidate School, in Newport, Rhode Island, in early June, 1952.

Navy OCS was one of the most difficult periods of my life; physically, mentally, and emotionally. In our first day there, candidates received a stack of textbooks which I was barely able to carry back to my barracks by extending my arms and hooking my fingertips under the bottom of the stack and tucking the top of the stack under my chin. We were told that all of the books would be covered during our four month course--and they were. The pressure was immense--lengthy assignments, frequent tests and an overriding threat that candidates who "bilged out" (failed) would be immediately sent to boot camp and then spend the remainder of their enlistment period as an enlisted person rather than an officer. I got to see my wife rarely and briefly. Fortunately, I survived and succeeded, and made a number of friends along the way. I graduated 8th out of a class of 684 candidates, and became an ensign in the United States Navy.

During the ensuing three years of active duty as a ground aircraft maintenance officer (not a pilot), I was sent to two specialists' schools where I learned the basics of navy aircraft maintenance and became a theoretical specialist in reciprocating engines and aircraft structures. Finally, I joined my duty squadron, VS-36, based in Norfolk, Virginia. VS-36 was an air-anti-submarine squadron whose mission was to detect enemy submarines and destroy them, or have them destroyed by surface warships. We embarked on a wide variety of aircraft carriers for training exercises and conducted a four month duty station assignment in the Mediterranean Sea, the latter beginning just four days after the birth of our first daughter. I was awarded a ribbon for service during the Korean Conflict, but was never shot at and was never sent west of the Mississippi River. I was honorably discharged from active duty in October, 1955, and narrowly escaped death in a crash landing of the navy plane which provided a ride home to my family in suburban Philadelphia.

I will be forever grateful for the maturation and lessons in leadership gained during my three years as a junior officer in the United States Navy. A generation later, my oldest son had a similar rewarding experience as a junior officer in the U.S. Coast Guard shortly after graduating from Wake Forest University. I would recommend similar expenditures of time for many young people who either encounter a need to serve their country or are not quite sure yet about what they want to do with their lives.

Employment opportunities were plentiful in the mid-1950s, and it was a "no brainer" decision for me to accept an offer from the Eastman Kodak Company in Rochester, New York. Assigned to the Camera Works Division, I started in industrial engineering, but was soon moved to a fast track training program which involved lengthy periods in accounting, wage and salary administration, and production and inventory control. My wife and I, and two daughters, settled in a pleasant suburb, became active in our church, and learned to enjoy northwestern New York State.

I might well have spent the rest of my working career with Kodak had not a college friend called me to see if I would be interested in the position of contract administrator at a small, rapidly expanding company located a few miles north of Princeton, New Jersey. This young organization had developed and patented an engineered material, comprised of fiberglass filament and epoxy resin, which had a tensile strength four times that of steel (on an equal weight basis), and possessed excellent dielectric and corrosion resistant properties. It had great potential for use in aeronautical applications (military and civilian) as well as a variety of electrical, structural, and safety products. I sensed an opportunity to quickly rise to a vice-presidential position and therefore left my excellent Kodak situation after 3 1/2 years, and moved to the warmer climate of central New Jersey. Just four months later, my new employer was acquired by Hercules Powder Company and I immediately changed from being " a big frog in a little puddle" to " a small frog in a big puddle".

Six years with Hercules were quite good however. The USSR had just put their Sputnik satellite in space, and America justifiably felt threatened. Our plant designed and manufactured strong, light weight rocket motor casings and nozzles for military purposes and NASA explorations; and I felt very good about being a part of this important effort. I became the plant superintendent and manager of technical services. (At that time, computers used punch cards and were the size of a big automobile). By 1965, the needs of the military and space organizations diminished, and our wonderful engineered material proved to be too costly for most civilian applications. I recognized that Hercules was predominantly a chemical organization, and that my future with them would now be rather limited. Therefore, I accepted a position with another company--this coming by way of a "head hunter" executive search firm.

I had begun studying for a Masters Degree in Business Administration at the University of Rochester, but my move to central New Jersey necessitated a change of schools. Therefore, I commuted evenings to Philadelphia and graduated with an MBA degree from Drexel Institute of Technology in 1962.

My next career stop was with the Polymer Corporation, in Reading, Pennsylvania. This company, privately held by an inventor/ principle owner and a few others, excelled in making engineered thermoplastic products from materials such as nylon, Teflon, acrylic, and polycarbonate--and variations thereof. Products included mill shapes, film, coatings, castings, and fabricated parts. I spent three years as production manager, working for a manufacturing executive who was a fine Christian man who believed in "quiet competence" and decency, but was unskilled in company politics.

During my last year at Polymer, the widow of the deceased inventor/ owner brought in an attorney to serve as president and groom the company for sale. Significant cost reduction efforts resulted in my superior being released, and I found myself among the favored higher level managers who survived. The atmosphere changed, however, from that of a thriving, growing, exciting firm to an uneasy organization, unsure of its future, and a group of individual managers looking out for "numero uno". Once again, I was ripe for a "head hunter" to call.

One should never flee, headlong and thoughtlessly, from a bad situation--but, that is exactly what I did, with disastrous results. I accepted a position as vice-president of manufacturing in a small, family-owned company in the food industry (which will remain unnamed). My title was prestigious and compensation was generous; however, I immediately found myself in a situation frought with serious problems including profitablity and cost, quality, scheduled deliveries, and safety--but without authority to make changes and spend money without the sole proprietor's approval, which was rarely forthcoming. It took me approximately four months to honorably "bail out" of this mess.

From the "help wanted" advertisements of a big city newspaper, I found and was selected for the position of plant manager of the Panelyte Division of the Thiokol Corporation, located in Trenton, New Jersey. Here, I was responsible for managing approximately 400 employees in a 365,000 square foot manufacturing facility. We made a wide variety of engineered thermoset plastic products, including printed circuit boards and laminates for many other purposes. A major achievement was to develop and market a new line of friction products, including disc brake pads for use in the automotive industry. During my two (+) years at Thiokol, the last of which I served as general manager-- unofficially filling the role of my prior boss who had been fired--we progressed from a discouraged, losing organization to a relatively happy, prideful, and profitable division. Unfortunately, however, the Panelyte Division did not fit in with Thiokol's long range plans and was headed for closure. At this point, I met the managing partner of the Management Advisory Services Division of the Philadelphia office of Price Waterhouse & Co., and he offered to have me join his firm as a management consultant. I snapped up the opportunity.

Thus began a ten year period of employment with a top-notch, highly ethical, professional organization in which I enjoyed a good feeling of serving client companies, and associating with a large number of fellow Price Waterhouse professionals, nationwide, for whom I developed the highest respect. Here, I was privileged to serve approximately fifty client organizations, mostly consulting in areas pertaining to operations and human resource management. Considerable travel was involved, and my clients included a wide variety of organizations--public and private sector, ranging from small to very large. Much satisfaction was gained from helping clients diagnose problems and find solutions.

After five years in the Philadelphia office of PW & Co, I was asked to move to the New York City office and assume administrative responsibilty for the firm's consulting practice in the northeastern quadrant of the United States. My family moved to Summit, New Jersey, a nice bedroom community from which I spent 1 1/2 hours per day commuting into Manhattan and another 1 1/2 hours per day returning home. Nevertheless, working in the "Big Apple" was both enjoyable and rewarding.

However, in the late 1970s, I was experiencing what some might call " mid-life crisis", wondering what God wanted me to do with the rest of my life; and it was then that I recognized the need and opportunity to improve the business and accounting programs taught at many of the Christian colleges in America.. Prayerful consideration, encouragement from some academic deans, and support from my wife led to my decision, at fifty years of age, to join the faculty of Taylor University.

My Price Waterhouse colleagues did not understand why I would accept a substantial reduction in compensation, and trade an outside window office, next to a corner of the 43rd floor of the Citicorp

Building, for a windowless "closet" office in academe. However, they gave me a standing ovation at my departure event and caused me to leave the firm with many good memories.

My time at Taylor University, located in a small community in central Indiana, began on a "downer" note. Four months after arriving, my first wife, Aileen, was diagnosed to be terminally ill with cancer-- undetected up to that point in her life. After a courageous four month battle, both prayerful and physical, Aileen passed away. I will always remember her being wheeled away, on a gurney, to her last operation from which she never regained consciousness. She was singing softly the old traditional hymn, "Have thine own way Lord, have thine own way..." Such was her faith.

I was left in a rather strange and difficult situation--starting a new career, 700 miles away from my home area, and responsible for a fifteen year old son (three other children were "out of the nest") and an aging mother-in-law who had come to live with us. With the help of a supportive Christian community (Taylor faculty and students and local townspeople) I managed to tough out a year of bereavement during which time I met, on a blind date, a wonderful Christian lady named Jane--divorced and a single mom with two kids--with whom, at this writing, I have enjoyed 27 years of a happy second marriage. God works in mysterious ways, his wonders to perform.

At Taylor, I was well received despite my lack of a PhD. My breadth of real world experience more than compensated for my not having "jumped through the hoops" required to receive a doctorate in my field of management. I got along very well with my students and most of the faculty and administrators, the latter sometimes viewing me as a bit too aggressive in pursuit of objectives and goals. In my teaching of the management subjects, I placed heavy emphasis on experiential learning; including field trips, guest speakers, case studies, practicums, a senior capstone trip to Chicago, and a semester-long Free Enterprise

Laboratory course for which I received an award from the Freedoms Foundation.

The Free Enterprise Laboratory course involved use of a vacant building and $60,000 in real money to allow three student teams to conceive (supported by a convincing business plan), run, and shut down three businesses--one in manufacturing, one in retailing, and one in consulting--hopefully breaking even or earning a surplus, although this did not always happen.

At the President's request, I became involved in strategic planning for the college--a rather frustrating experience as I tried to share business principles and practices with committee members from other academic disciplines.

All told, my fifteen years at Taylor were very rewarding. When I left PW&Co to join the Taylor faculty, my colleagues joked that I was heading into semi-retirement at an early age. How wrong they were. I had always worked hard, but never as long and hard as I did at Taylor. Believing in Taylor's mission and my own vision to create Christian Tigers, I found there to be no end of important things to do, albeit with limited help and funding. Such is the case in many of the smaller, private colleges.

Taylor is a fine school, regularly ranking in the top three regional liberal arts colleges in the midwest (U S News and World Report annual rankings). While there, I heard many of America's most highly respected evangelical Christian speakers share in Taylor's chapel programs. (Students were expected--but not absolutely required--to attend chapel services, and they did attend because they wanted to.) I developed the highest respect for Taylor's outstanding student development program, and for most of the faculty whose dedication to the students resulted in a very high percentage earning their bachelors degree diplomas in four years.

I engaged in some political battles with some administrators (yes, politics rears its head in all types of organizations--even Christian), and didn't always win, even when I was proven to be right. Nevertheless, I had an opportunity to impact the lives of more than a thousand students, most of whom are, or will be, making a difference for good in the world.

Hearing loss, fatigue, and short-term memory problems--all of which come with aging--impair my ability to now teach in a traditional sense. However, I have a continuing desire to share important elements of the non-textbook wisdom and experiences I have gained during my lifetime. I have not been a super star, but I have been blessed with a successful career which has been filled with a wide variety of experiences--some good and some bad--many of which illustrate timeless principles which should be useful to maturing students and young professionals as they pursue success within Judeo-Christian ethical guidelines. Sharing these "gems" of wisdom and experience is the purpose of this book. I hope you find it useful and enjoyable.

# Choosing a College--Some Important but Less Obvious Factors to Consider

College is a <u>huge investment</u>--four or more years of your life and mega bucks for tuition, room, board, and expenses; the latter coming from sacrificing parents, scholarships, and/or your own earnings and indebtedness. This 5% of your lifetime should be an enjoyable, challenging period of growth. It should not be thought of as a "rite of passage" from youth to adulthood which can be devoted primarily to play. I have seen too many young people enter college with no idea about their future, play around during much or all of their college years, and sometimes graduate with still no awareness of what they want to do--except perhaps to get married. In our "shrunken" world, populated by millions of highly competitive young people who previously lacked opportunity but now have it, it is vital for young folks to <u>get serious sooner</u>, and for parents, teachers and coaches to help them do so. An important step is for students to <u>choose their college wisely</u>.

Current literature is replete with basic advice such as: (1) formulate some type of career goals and how best to prepare for such; (2) use the many publications which identify colleges by location, majors offered, and ratings; (3) start serious considerations during your junior year in high school, and visit prospective campuses during the summer vacation between junior and senior years; (4) don't procrastinate in submitting applications to targeted schools; (5) research comparative costs and financial aid availabilities; (6) explore and pursue all available scholarship opportunities for which you might be a successful applicant/candidate; etc..

The foregoing are obvious, albeit often ignored, suggestions. What follows are deeper, less widely discussed observations and ideas stemming from my experience as a student, parent, and college professor and administrator.

Decide to <u>live on campus</u> during your undergraduate education if you can afford to do so. Campus life is an enjoyable, enriching, maturing experience which is far preferable to the relative drudgery of commuting. In retrospect, despite having enjoyed a good experience as a commuter student at Drexel University, I regret having chosen Drexel over a top rated engineering school in upstate New York (250 miles away from my home in suburban Philadelphia) to which I was accepted with a scholarship. I missed the opportunity to learn from four years of semi-independent living, to become more involved in campus activities, and to establish a network of lifelong friends. Continued living at home did allow me to put myself through college financially; but, socially, I did not break away from home until I experienced the harsh reality of Officer Candidate School--which caused me to mature in a hurry.

Location-wise, other factors being somewhat equal, I would recommend choosing a college between 250-400 miles from home--making trips home and parental visits reasonably easy, but discouraging undue frequency.

<u>Campus visits</u> are a very important element in your decision process. Summer tours are OK, but visiting during the traditional nine month school year is preferable--during which time you can see the entire operation from a prospective participant's point of view. Most colleges have well planned, well rehearsed visitation programs to present to

prospective students and their parents. If possible, it would be desirable to dig deeper than the canned presentation--perhaps even arranging an overnight stay in a dormitory.

From an academic perspective, you should try to meet at least two professors in your field(s) of interest, exploring not only their expertise but also their genuine interest and ability in teaching at the undergraduate level. There are many faculty members, holding doctorates, who are true scholars; but, there are some who have gotten their required doctoral credentials at lower quality institutions without undergoing the rigorous study and research traditionally associated with a PhD degree--thereby satisfying requirements to attain tenure and be counted as a doctor in the comparative/competitive ratings of colleges and universities. In some cases, faculty with respected masters degrees coupled with extensive experience in their field(s) may be outstanding teachers at the undergraduate level.

Similarly, explore university policies regarding requiring professors responsible for courses to actually teach in the classrooms and not delegate such instruction to graduate assistants. This occurs, with disturbing frequency, at some large institutions where highly skilled professors busy themselves with research and writing for publication to the detriment of students who deserve greater exposure to the university's top talent. Granted, faculty members are expected to stay at the "cutting edge" in their respective disciplines and "publish or perish" in their career paths toward promotion and tenure. Also, it is understandable that highly educated, widely respected professors may become frustrated and bored dealing with undergraduate college students, particularly in the lower level courses. Nevertheless, you students are paying for and deserve a top notch education, and it is the faculty's primary responsibility to provide such while still engaging in appropriate research and writing. I am proud to have been associated with two universities, one small and one large, where the professors were always in the classrooms.

Academic advising systems and student/faculty relationships are also areas to be thoroughly explored. Course selection and scheduling are vital ingredients in helping students optimize their college experience and graduate (with bachelors degrees in most majors) in four years or less. Yes, eighteen year old students might be expected to think clearly and successfully plan their own academic programs--but, many do not, and parents are often not much help. Ideally, a faculty advisor should be assigned to each student at the outset of his/her college career, with this relationship continuing until graduation unless, of course, the student changes majors in which case an appropriate change of advisors would be desirable.

Students have a way of placing high priorities on taking courses and/or professors perceived to be easier,(e.g. Biology vs. Physics, and American History vs. World History), and which are scheduled at more convenient times. Skilled, friendly, concerned advisors are sometimes needed to strongly urge advisees to do what is best for them. My oldest son spent four years at a prestigious southern university without a concerned, knowledgeable advisor (and without adequate coaching from me) and graduated with a bachelors degree in a major for which there was almost zero employment marketability. Fortunately, he was accepted into Coast Guard Officers' Candidate School, became an officer, served six years in the Coast Guard, and is now engaged in a successful career in health care. I'm very proud of my son, but his college years could have been more fruitful--and effective advising could have been the key.

Find a way to talk with some students, not just those who are tour guides. This might best be accomplished by spending a night in a dormitory and experiencing campus food service. Ask about social life, hopefully offering fun and friendships in a wholesome manner (organizations, dormitory wings, fraternities, sororities, parties, concerts, etc.). How do students feel about the faculty and administration? Is there opportunity for spiritual growth and sharing on campus or in the city or nearby towns? What are the behavioral standards and expectations? How is school spirit--are students proud to be a part of their college?

Also, be alert and observe on your own the general culture existing on campus--friendly and open vs. impersonal, student attire, diversity vs. uniformity of population, attitudes toward religion, etc. Be aware that much of the social maturation you experience during your college years will reflect relationships with friends and peers, hopefully leading to wholesome growth and lifelong friendships. Much of your learning will involve fellow students. The best schools generally attract the best students.

Of course, extra-curricular activities are an important element in college life. Find out what is available. There should be a number of appealing activities and organizations regardless of what your interests and talents are. Hopefully, you will want to stay on campus most weekends instead of retreating to your home base.

Taylor University, where I served for fifteen years, is located "out in the sticks". However, it has a very friendly culture and an outstanding array of student activities which cause most students to enjoy staying on campus or traveling with friends to nearby communities during weekends in the school year. Beyond that, a very effective advising system results in a high student retention rate and most students graduating in four years or less. This, in turn, leads to high alumni loyalty and support. These factors play a significant role in causing Taylor to be repeatedly ranked among the top three liberal arts colleges in the mid-west. Such factors should also be considered in your choice of targeted schools.

One more thing you might not normally think of: Check out the presence and effectiveness of each school's career guidance and placement operation. They should be able to provide psychological and aptitude testing, knowledgeable counseling, internship opportunities, and introductions to job placement opportunities upon graduation.

Find out what organizations interview on campus, for recruitment purposes, and what percentage of graduates are employed in fields of their choice shortly after graduation. Also, learn about whatever placement services are offered to alumni. For those considering additional education beyond the bachelor's degree level, try to learn how successful graduates of colleges you are exploring have been in gaining admittance to graduate programs you may want to pursue.

Perhaps the most important thing you might learn from this chapter is how to create and use a Weighted Factor Matrix as a tool in helping you make a sound choice of a college, or colleges, from the larger number of candidate schools which you started exploring. The logical process is very simple. Start by identifying the factors which are of varying degrees of importance to you. e.g. college reputation, cost, location, living conditions, campus culture, food service, etc. Then, assign relative numerical weights to each factor, indicating the relative importance of each factor, e.g. very important, important, nice to have but not vital, not a factor in decision making. Then, using a matrix format as shown in Figure (1), give each candidate school a raw numerical score in each factor, e. g. outstanding, very good, average, below average, poor. Multiply the raw scores for each factor by the assigned weights for the factors, thereby creating weighted scores for each factor at each candidate school. Adding the weighted factor scores for each college yields a composite weighted score which can be used for comparison purposes.

Such Weighted Factor Matrices can be useful in making decisions in many walks of life, e.g. choosing among employment possibilities, selecting a house, deciding upon a retirement location, or even choosing a girl friend or boy friend to seriously pursue. Of course, the resulting numerical scores will not automatically dictate a decision. "Gut feel" and other emotional issues are also very important. However, the discipline of thinking through the listing of important factors and their relative weights, and then scoring candidates in each factor. leading to comparative composite weighted scores, can be nothing but helpful in your decision making process.

To repeat: College is a huge investment. Get serious sooner, and make the decision wisely.

*Figure 1*

WEIGHTED FACTOR MATRIX
(CHOICE OF COLLEGES)

| FACTOR | FACTOR WEIGHT* | Candidate Institutions | | | | | | | |
| | | Alpha | | Beta | | Delta | | Epsilon | |
| | | Raw Score** | Weighted Score | Raw Score | Weighted Score | Raw Score | Weighted Score | Raw Score | Weighted Score |
|---|---|---|---|---|---|---|---|---|---|
| College reputation | 2 | 3 | 6 | 1 | 2 | 1 | 2 | 3 | 6 |
| Academic reputation in major | 2 | 2 | 4 | 2 | 4 | 1 | 2 | 1 | 2 |
| Cost (affordability) | 3 | 0 | 0 | 2 | 6 | 1 | 3 | 1 | 3 |
| Location | 1 | 1 | 1 | 3 | 3 | 3 | 3 | 1 | 1 |
| Living conditions | 2 | 3 | 6 | 1 | 2 | 1 | 2 | 2 | 4 |
| Food service | 2 | 2 | 4 | 1 | 2 | 1 | 2 | 2 | 4 |
| Advising | 2 | 2 | 4 | 2 | 4 | 1 | 2 | 1 | 2 |
| Extra curricular activities | 2 | 3 | 6 | 2 | 4 | 1 | 2 | 2 | 4 |
| Placement services | 1 | 2 | 2 | 1 | 1 | 1 | 1 | 2 | 2 |
| Campus culture | 3 | 1 | 3 | 3 | 9 | 0 | 0 | 0 | 0 |

Total weighted scores     <u>36</u>     <u>37</u>     <u>19</u>     <u>28</u>

*Factor Weights : 3 = very important
2 = important
1 = nice to have, but not vital
0 = not a factor in decision making

**Raw Scores : 3 = outstanding
2 = very good
1 = average
0 = below average
-1 = poor

# The College Years--Make the Most of Them

<u>Select a major  (and minors) wisely and pursue them vigorously.</u> Yes, college years provide opportunities to mature (often living away from home for the first time), make new friends (hopefully good ones which will last a lifetime), and have fun. <u>However</u>, remember the huge investment of time and money being made by you and your parents and other supporters, and make the most of it in preparing for a rewarding and God pleasing career and life.

Understandably, many (maybe most)  freshmen are unsure of themselves and where they should be headed, <u>but</u> that is not an excuse for procrastinating about getting serious. The freshman year can afford students an opportunity to get a handle on themselves while taking selected general education courses which are required at most good quality schools. Learn to write and speak well, including public presentations. Literature, college mathematics, and science courses will help you develop skills in critical, logical, quantitative thinking. Becoming proficient in one or more foreign languages is very important, as is gaining a better appreciation of world history and cultures. Also, don't brush off the fine arts (classical music, theater, and art). When you graduate into careers which require a college education, you will be

8

expected to be at least conversant about the traditional arts which have survived centuries of fads which come and go.

During my undergraduate time, shortly after World War ll, I earned a degree in industrial engineering but took just one general education course--English Composition. Such a narrow approach to college education is not tolerated in most college programs today. Fortunately, I had acquired good reading, writing, and quantitative skills in high school, and by growing up in a well-educated family with cultural interests. Many kids are not so blessed. Also, believe it or not, regular church attendance helped build vocabulary as did listening to news broadcasts (Lowell Thomas, Edward R. Murrow, etc). Reading newspapers and library books also helped.

Take advantage of guest lecturers coming to campus, chapel services, and artists' series which may feature various forms of music, theater, and art. Students often give low priority to such events unless they present performers and performances which are currently popular (faddish). To prod students to take advantage of what is offered, professors often must resort to requiring proof of attendance--either via punched cards or questions on tests related to suggested/required presentations external to the classroom. Again, remember that you and your family are paying dearly for these privileges, even if you do not consider them such at the time. I've often seen students attend required presentations, get their attendance card or ticket punched, and then leave at intermission-- hoping that they wont be asked questions pertaining to the second half of the performance. What a shame!

In a more upbeat situation, while approaching the auditorium at Ball State University to attend a classical concert, I once observed a large number of young men and their dates leaving one of the most prestigious fraternities on campus voluntarily to attend the concert. During intermission, I asked a few of the fraternity brothers what brought them to this classical event. Their reply was that they just thought it might be a neat thing to do, and it turned out that way, and they were staying for the second half.

To summarize: General education courses are an important part of your education which will help you grow as a well rounded person, capable of thinking and acting beyond the relatively narrow scopes of your chosen specialties. Appreciate and enjoy them.

Next, a word about the desirability of developing a balanced lifestyle during your college years. Well-run fraternities and sororities, and other organizations (both social and purpose-driven), can be very beneficial in building lifelong friendships, improving social skills, and providing opportunities to learn and practice managerial/leadership skills. Intramural sports competition allows many folks who may not be varsity-caliber athletes to participate in wholesome physical activities. Also, while dating is to be encouraged, try to keep romance and courtships in perspective despite the hormonal rush which is quite normal in this time of life. Hopefully, such relationships will not preclude development in academics and extra-curricular activities.

Also, seek experiential learning opportunities as much as possible. Internships, practicums, and general summer employment will provide exposure to the real world and enhance the wisdom and sensitivity with which you view things. Ball State University has recently adopted a slogan/tagline, "education redefined". This is based on a principle of immersive learning wherein every BSU student will engage in at least one real world project appropriate to his/her major/interests. Similarly, At Taylor University, the Business Department's Free Enterprise Laboratory was a very useful learning experience for students and earned national recognition and an award from the Freedoms Foundation

<u>Begin thinking (soon) and planning for the rest of your life</u>-- leading to selection of a major(s), minor(s), and courses. Preferably, this should be done no later than early in your sophomore year. You might say that you still don't know what you want to do in life, but that is not a good excuse for continuing to drift. It is far better to plan

and then change the plan than not to plan at all. Toward that end, it is good to seek advice from family, faculty advisors, and professional counselors in the college's career development department; and, adopt an organized approach to planning. The Strategic Planning Process is very effective for organizations and people. A logical approach for an individual person follows.

The ancient Greek philosopher, Socrates, is credited with saying, "Know thyself". Who are you and why are you here? Understanding yourself and your purpose in life are vital beginning points in developing a plan for your life. Many parents (not all) are very capable and willing to help you think this through--if you will listen and appreciate what they have to offer. However, many undergraduate students tend to shake off the influence of their parents now that they are living away from home and "on their own (?)". Here is where faculty advisors and mentors can play an important role if their institution encourages such, and if they can find time to truly relate to their advisees in addition to teaching, committee work, and satisfying the "publish or perish" syndrome which afflicts many dedicated professors. The presence of a sound student advising system should be thoroughly checked out as part of your college selection process.

Professionally staffed campus career development organizations can also be very helpful--first by guiding you through a variety of psychological, personality, and aptitude tests; and then helping you become more aware of what opportunities are "out there"; followed by helping you match your skills, characteristics, and interests with appropriate careers. Assuming you target some semi-specific goals and work toward them, career development departments should also be very helpful in helping you find internships/practicums during your college years, and subsequently aiding you in gaining appropriate full-time employment upon graduation. Good career development organizations will also provide assistance to alumni seeking to change employers and/or career paths sometime after graduation.

Once you have achieved a reasonably realistic understanding of yourself, it is time to address the question of why God gave you life and put you here. What are the big, broad, over-arching purposes of your life?. In the broadest of terms, the Westminster Catechism of the Presbyterian Church offers the rhetorical question: "What is the chief and highest end of man (people)?" with the rhetorical response being: "The chief and highest end of man (people) is to glorify God and fully to enjoy Him forever." This speaks to using your earthly life, time, and talents in ways pleasing to, and perhaps directed by, God.

There are countless ways to pursue this macro mission in your life. You do not necessarily have to be a pastor, missionary, physician, teacher, nun, etc., nor do you have to live in poverty to satisfy God's wishes for your life. You can become an engineer, scientist, lawyer, farmer, craftsperson, assembler, actor, athlete, truck driver, retailer, cook, soldier, laborer, etc..as long as you are using your God-given talents in pursuit of worthy goals, ranging from survival to top level leadership and professionalism. Of course, things like prostitution, pornography and dealing in drugs would hardly be deemed acceptable.

Is attainment of a high ranking, highly compensated position--gained via fair competition--to be considered sinful ? Certainly not if the motivation for such achievement is to use talents and time to do good, including acceptance of the rewards which attend success; and not selfish greed, ego, and lust for power. To many people, Jimmy Carter exemplifies a relatively humble person who used his talents and efforts honorably (albeit not always successfully) to become, for four years, the most powerful person in the world. On the other end of the spectrum of successful Christian lives is Mother Teresa who (although extremely talented) lived in self-imposed poverty while she ministered personally to thousands of destitute people and spiritually to millions of other folks.

While teaching at Taylor University, I was responsible for bringing a significant number of high ranking business executives to campus to share their experiences, advice, and Christian faith with students and the local community. On one occasion, the CEO of a large corporation, listed in the New York Stock Exchange, had finished giving his prepared talk to a large group of business students and was fielding questions from the audience. A young man, brought up in a fundamentalist congregation, publicly asked our CEO guest how he could feel good about himself wearing very expensive clothing, e.g. Brooks Brothers' suit and Florsheim shoes, when he could dress himself at much lower cost and donate the monetary difference to feeding the poor. This student's distasteful question was the source of much embarrassment and reflected a gross misunderstanding of the need for high level executives to dress and behave like high level executives in order to fulfill their responsibilities. This CEO did not live ostentatiously and gave generously to his church and other charitable causes. I was ashamed of my student's behavior and hope that his opinion that wealth is automatically synonymous with sin is not shared by many within the Christian persuasion.

Self analysis prepares you to develop a more specific, personalized mission statement for your own life. (It helps to write it down and not just dream about it.) Mission statements, organizational or individual, should be brief but very thoroughly thought through; and they should serve as general guidelines for a significant portion of your life--again applying to both corporate and individual lives. Yes, mission statements can be changed, but hopefully only after much thought.

Many decades ago, most business organizations considered their primary mission to be maximization of profit, preferably within the constraints of the law, but without too much regard for fair treatment of their employees, suppliers, customers, and community. Today, enlightened executives and managers are much more broadly attentive to the needs of their entire spectrum of stakeholders (not just stockholders). Stakeholders include owners/principals of the organization (stockholders), but also include workers, customers and clients, suppliers, and the public at large. Broad issues to sincerely consider might include: providing consistent top value for customers; encouraging, empowering, and enabling employees to better themselves and find satisfaction in their work; maintaining fair dealings with suppliers; contributing to community well-being via taxes and voluntary involvement; achieving and maintaining innovative, technical superiority; etc.

Written succinctly and with brevity, such corporate mission statements are printed and distributed, and become the general guidelines within which an organization functions.

In the case of individuals, it is also good and useful to develop a mission statement reflecting personalized, general goals and guidelines for living your life. For the Christian, the Parable of the Talents (Matthew 25: 14-30), dealing with good stewardship of what is entrusted to you; and Rick Warren's book, The Purpose Driven Life, are good starting points for your thought process.

Every person will have a different approach to developing a lifetime mission statement. Some will anticipate working primarily in order to exist (hopefully with beneficial, enjoyable sideline activities). Others, at the opposite extreme, will live to work (thoroughly enjoying careers, sometimes to the detriment of family life.) My mother, wife of a very dedicated pastor, occasionally accused my father of being married to the church rather than her--not good. Most folks will see themselves somewhere between these two extremes; but, in all cases, some sound, general mission principles deserve careful thought and adoption-- allocating time and effort to career, family, and church/community endeavors

One large, successful business organization has a motto, "To honor God in all we do". This could well be adopted by individuals as they plan for their future and lifetime activity. The Ten Commandments is another valuable set of principles to live by. Other, more specific yet general, guidelines might include:

- Living by the Golden Rule in all aspects of life
- Enjoying, and committing to, a loving, lifetime marriage
- Raising a family of capable, honest, caring, and competitive (in a good sense) children
- Serving as a citizen, in ways both large and/or small, to local community, country, and world
- Exercising truth, integrity, and fairness in all dealings--corporate and private
- Continuing to learn and grow--using your God-given talents, time, and health to the best of your ability

OK, you may say that such mission statement issues are pretty bland; but, remember that they are general guidelines and, as such, they are very important. Next we come to considering vision(s).

In a planning sense, visions are "big picture" dreams of what you would like to see happen in the future-short term, intermediate term, and long term. They can, again, be both corporate and individual; and they can/should generate <u>excited</u> effort by organizations and people as they strive to fulfill the dream(s)--even though the odds might seem to be heavily stacked against achieving such success.

Vision(s) provide motivation--again both corporate and individual. Psychologist Abraham Maslow's "hierarchy of needs" theory lists the following human needs in increasing order of importance:
- Physiological/survival
- Security/safety
- Acceptance
- Esteem--self and from others
- Self-actualization--to use one's potential to the fullest and achieve something worthwhile

Pursuing, and hopefully achieving, visions fits well with satisfying the "esteem" and "self-actualization" needs identified by Maslow--

assuming that the first three human needs have first been met. The excited, creative efforts generated by important, attractive visions will often lead to highly desirable results; and even if the total vision is not fully attained, many beneficial gains will normally be achieved along the way.

The absence of visions and goals can lead to complacency, disinterest, poor choices, and decline (again both corporate and individual). The Bible states this very cryptically in Proverbs 29:18. "Where there is no vision, the people perish" (King James Version), or "Where there is no vision, the people run wild" (Living Bible). Complacency is a dangerous way of living--for individuals, schools, churches, business organizations, communities, and nations.

Organizational/societal visions usually start with a leader who is able to skillfully share his/her dream with followers and then cause them to excitedly and effectively pursue the dream to fruition. Some examples are: Martin Luther King's vision of ending racial segregation and achieving racial equality; Nelson Mandela's dream of ending apartheid in South Africa; Millard Fuller's concept of providing adequate housing via the Habitat for Humanity organization; Adolph Hitler's dream of establishing Aryan supremacy throughout Europe and the world (not a good vision but nonetheless effectively pursued for many years); Rotary International's vision of stamping out polio thoroughout the world; and a Christian college's dream of earning a top ten national ranking while holding to the Christian beliefs and principles on which it was founded.

I, personally, did not have a mission statement for my life, nor any visions to pursue when I graduated from college and continued through part of my career in the Navy and civilian manufacturing management. An increasing desire to serve caused me to enter the management consulting profession, and this ultimately led me to join Taylor University as a professor of management and chairperson of the Business, Accounting, and Economics Department. Here, I developed a personal and departmental vision of improving the Department to a point of being recognized as the best Business Department within the Christian College Coalition (a loose organization of more than 70 Christian colleges in the USA). Our faculty worked very hard and effectively, and succeeded, at that time, in gaining the favorable reputation we sought.

Returning to the issue of self analysis, it would have been wise if I had known and utilized an organizational analytical procedure identified by the acronym, "SWOT". This applies to you today just as much as it should have to me years ago. "SWOT" stands for: Strengths, Weaknesses, Opportunities, and Threats. To these categories, I would add one more--Interests--for people who are in a career planning stage.

The strength category pertains not to good characteristics which you may have, but which you probably share with thousands of other folks in your peer group, e.g. intelligent, personable, healthy. Rather, in our competitive society, it is important that you recognize the unique characteristics, with which you have been blessed, which allow you to stand out above the crowd. Here, one might consider specific knowledge, experiences, skills, learning capabilities, physical strengths, etc.. Examples might be: fluency in one or more foreign languages; familiarity with one or more foreign cultures; leadership experiences; unique work experiences; recognized skills in music, technology, teaching, communication, etc.. Such factors are those which gives one a competitive advantage in the employment marketplace.

At the same time, it is important that you recognize characteristics in which you are weak relative to other people. Such awareness might cause you to accept these personal shortcomings and avoid careers and employment situations wherein you would be at a disadvantage. Or, you might choose to find ways to overcome recognized weaknesses, thereby allowing you to more effectively pursue desired visions and goals. Examples of competitive weaknesses are: poor communication skills; obesity; poor grades and lack of meaningful experiences; lack of favorable personal references; etc.. Some disadvantages are natural and impossible to overcome--and must be lived with. Even here, however, many examples can be found of severely disadvantaged people who have found ways to work, serve, and lead rewarding lives. During my time at Taylor University, I learned to admire a young man who had been stricken with polio and became a quadriplegic, living on a gurney. Nonetheless, he became a skilled, employed computer programmer and an avid fan at athletic events. He was an inspiration to all who encountered him. On the other hand, many competitive weaknesses, such as those mentioned in the foregoing examples, can and should be overcome if necessary to successfully pursue a worthwhile vision/career.

The Strengths and Weaknesses elements in the SWOT acronym reflect factors which are peculiar to you and which you can do something about. Opportunities and Threats are elements, relative to your mission, vision, and interests, which you can do nothing about but which will probably affect your future life. Opportunities should be recognized and ways should be found to take advantage of such. For example: our aging population will require increasing care (medical, pastoral, economic, and social); globalization presents huge marketing opportunities; goods will continue to need to be transported; growing shortages in pastoral and teaching professions will need to be filled; nanotechnology will enter more and more aspects of our lives; homelend security and pursuit of peace throughout the world will demand increasing levels of skilled, dedicated people in public and military service. These foregoing issues are quite broad albeit correct. You would do well to focus attention on more specific opportunities related to your specific vision, strengths, and interests. Also to be considered is what is most important to you--getting wealthy as quickly as possible or serving your God and the people around you. These goals are not necessarily mutually exclusive.

As this is being written, there is a huge demand for health care practioners, accountants, truck drivers, teachers of mathematics and science, and American engineers and scientists. Globalization/outsourcing has taken a big toll, in the more highly developed countries, of job opportunities in manufacturing, information processing, and routine communications. Various types of business and professions have risen and fallen in recent years. Biotechnology, energy, environmental issues, finance, and marketing are some of the areas experiencing growth while we see declining employment opportunities in agriculture, plastics, and retail stores to name a few.

Volumes could be written on the subject of Opportunities and Threats, but that is not the objective of this book. It is vitally important, however, that you--college students, young professionals, and concerned parents become and stay aware of what is going on in the world around you, and specifically how trends and events will affect you and your future. Too many college students and some newly minted graduates are content to view college--and some post-college time-- as a period of entitled play. Refusing to grow up, such young people defy my plea for them to "Get serious sooner", and consequently fail to prepare for coming opportunities and/or find themselves handicapped or defeated by not anticipating looming threats. Good places to start upgrading awareness include serious reading of serious news publications, serious viewing of TV and internet, and serious discussions with friends and peers.

Today's macro threats include increased global competition, educational deficiencies in America, growing national debt and unfavorable balance of payments in commerce with other countries, terrorism, environmental concerns, increasing bankruptcies and debtors unable to pay large credit card obligations, decreasing interest in patriotism, morality and religion, and increasing time spent in non-productive communication and play. Of course, taking action to correct some of these threats presents opportunities.

Micro threats might be issues such as competition moving into your area, deteriorating infrastructure and increasing taxes in your community, being overtaken by technological improvements, difficulty in recruiting talented employees due to location and/or compensation constraints, etc.

OK, Now that you have done a thorough job of recognizing who you are, thinking about your personal mission and vision(s), and performing a SWOT analysis of yourself and your environment, you should have a pretty good picture of where you are at the present time, and where you would like to be at some time in the future. You are now ready to develop a plan for getting there--fulfilling your mission and achieving your vision(s).

In my career, I really had no plan until I was in my late 40s. Fortunately, I had enjoyed success because I had worked hard and well--but, essentially, I was lucky to have good opportunities just open themselves up for me. Or, maybe God had a hand in preparing me to teach and lead at Taylor University. I guess I'll never know the answer to that question until God accepts me into Heaven--as bad as I have been and still am. Nevertheless, I have admired folks who knew where they were going in their careers and were able to pursue an organized approach to achieving their goals.

In particular, I am thinking of a talented, personable, ethical principal in the Management Consulting Practice,at Price Waterhouse, who was elected to that rank at a relatively early age. Upon graduating from college, he knew exactly what he wanted to achieve and how to go about it--first getting hired as a staff consultant and then rapidly earning promotion through the ranks of senior consultant, manager, senior manager, and then principal (equivalent to the rank of partner in the Accounting Practice). Early on, he learned what needed to be done and did it, i.e. performing quality work at increasing levels of complexity, charging a large number of consulting hours for which the firm could bill clients, writing articles for magazines and professional journals, giving speeches, engaging successfully in professional practice development (a euphemism for selling engagements), joining and assuming leadership in civic organizations, joining a country club and playing golf well, being highly ethical in all his doings, and developing friendly relationships at all levels within the firm.

Such planning and doing is possible--indeed advisable--in most career paths/walks of life, rather than just taking whatever comes along. "Impossible !" you may say. "It is well known that many/most people change jobs and career paths many times during their lives. Why spend time, energy, and worry on things that will likely change in my life ?" To this, I say that it is always better to have planned and then changed--due to choice or necessity--than to have not planned at all.

Now that you've completed your "big picture" thinking (missions and visions), and done "homework" regarding your interests, what unique talents you have to offer, what you might want to avoid, and the nature of your environment, you are ready for the more detailed aspects of planning--establishing objectives, strategies, tactics, and tasks which will help you achieve what you want to do with the rest of your life.

Some definitions might be helpful here. I, personally, have experienced organizational committees, charged with creating a strategic plan, wasting countless hours arguing over semantics, e.g. whether certain issues are objectives, policies, practices, programs, etc. What a frustrating waste of time ! For simplicity purposes, let us agree to use the following definitions.

Objectives--deal with relatively important, "big picture", targeted achievements. They deal with what must be completed, when it must be done, and by whom (establishing overall responsibility). Objectives should be as specific and verifiable as possible, e.g complete course work in masters degree program before beginning thesis work; get thesis topic approved and complete research; write thesis and have it approved by advisor and committee; graduate with masters degree. In this illustration, you, the graduate student, are the responsible party. In a corporate setting, certain managers can be held responsible for objectives charged to a group.

Objectives can be both long term and short term. The shorter term planning will naturally incorporate more detailed planning regarding specific strategies, tactics, programs, and tasks. Each of these, with the exception of some strategies, should have a well-defined time line indicating a definite beginning date and targeted completion time.

A word about time is appropriate here. Time is an extremely valuable asset in a person's life. We are given, on average, 78(+) years to live. That breaks down into months, weeks, days, and even minutes. As these elements of time pass, they are gone forever and are irretrievable. Therefore, you should carefully consider how you will allocate time to various aspects of your life (more about this later) and how to use time efficiently (doing the things right) and effectively (doing the right things).

Fifty (+) years ago, a British historian, Northcote Parkinson, published an observation which became known as Parkinson's Law-- "Work expands to fill the time allowed for its completion". This applies today to the scheduling of completion dates for objectives and supporting programs and tasks. If you target a challenging but achievable date, you will probably get the work done in the allowable time frame. However, if you allow a more relaxed time to achieve something, the work will probably consume that entire amount of time. Therefore, a fairly tight but realistic schedule of actvities and supporting step completions is advisable, both for individuals and organizations, if performance is to be optimized.

Strategies--define, in broad terms, how different objectives are to be pursued. They represent overarching philosophies and policies which can relate to large scale objectives and/or shorter term tactics and tasks. They do not necessarily specify verifiable, quantitative results or finite timetables.

For example, after the early military victories in the Iraq war, America and its allies had macro objectives of rebuilding the country's infrastructure and creating a democracy-type government which would encourage and permit Shiites, Sunnis, and Kurds to work and live together in a peaceful environment. A major <u>strategy</u> promoting this was to win the hearts and minds of the Iraqi people, which has turned out to be only partially successful at this writing.

On the corporate/business level, strategies may range from the small entrepreneur finding small niche business opportunities where there are few, if any, competitors--to gigantic organizations such as Walmart whose strategy is manifest in its motto, " Low Prices-Always". Emphasis on establishing comprehensive discount stores in smaller communities was/is another important strategy of Walmart.

On an individual basis, strategies can be both general and specifically related to personal objectives. For example: during college years, aim to take the most beneficial courses even though they might be taught by demanding professors at early or late times of the day; develop broad, extra-curricular experiences (athletics, music, publications, student government, etc.); establish a sizeable group of lifelong friends who you will be happy to help or be helped by; use summer work experiences to continue learning and growing; do whatever it takes to maintain spirituality and grow in this important aspect of life; and live frugally, negating or minimizing accumulation of debt.

Young professionals who aspire to lofty positions would do well to join and participate in civic, professional, and religious organizations--and, in so doing, develop friends and contacts, and earn a favorable reputation.

The subject of <u>tactics, programs, and tasks</u> can be lumped together for discussion purposes. They are more finite in nature and, often in your career path, will be related to and supportive of your mission, visions, objectives, and strategies--or they may be merely assignments which, nevertheless, need to be completed succesfully. Here, some very detailed planning is important--with specific task completions (results, dates, and responsible parties) clearly spelled out. Illustrations of such tactics, programs, and tasks are:

- Military: Find and destroy Al Qaeda terrorist group now launching rockets from a certain city in Iraq.
  Do this in the next five days. Assigned to Company B under Captain Jones.
- Corporate: Reduce inventory levels by 20% within the new fiscal year. Responsibility of Industrial
  Engineering and Materials Management team under Ronald Smart
- Student: Produce award winning weekly college newspaper by competition date. Responsibility of senior editor.
- Young Professional: Earn respected masters degree no later than six years after graduating with bachelors degree. Responsibility: Self

In the planning for specific tactics, programs, and tasks, it is important to answer, or be able to answer, the six "magic" questions: what?, when?, where?, how?, who?, and why?. Answers to these questions and other considerations should be written down and not be dependent on memory.

Tasks and supportive sub-tasks can then be organized into a time-related program plan which lists the activities necessary to complete the assigned tactic/program (or objective on a larger scale). Sophisticated, highly skilled planners of complex projects, such as designing and building a new weapons system, are fond of using computerized planning tools such as PERT (Program Evaluation and Review Technique) and CPM (Critical Path Method) to not only plan but also continually review actual progress in comparison with the plan. A planning tool which is much simpler and easier to understand is the

Gantt Chart, developed during World War l by Henry L. Gantt, a revered pioneer in industrial engineering and management consultant.

Gantt Charts are widely used today, either on computer or with paper and pencil, and they are readily understood by anyone with a high school diploma. Essentially, such charts list all of the key activities involved in a project/program. Beside each activity listed, on a time-oriented grid, bars are drawn to show expected beginning dates, elapsed time for completion, and necessary completion dates (sometimes depicted by a symbol such as a triangle).

Attention is given to each activity's starting and ending dates relative to other activities which might have to be completed first and/or other subsequent activities which are dependent on the activity being entered in the plan. Room can be provided on a Gantt Chart to show who is responsible for each activity, and sometimes even the activity costs and benefits involved.

Gantt Charts permit a project leader, or an individual, to periodically check actual progress vs. each planned activity and either take corrective action to force delinquent tasks to meet the plan, or revise the plan to reflect reality.

To illustrate the simplistic effectiveness of Gantt Charts, I have chosen to show imaginary planning for an event/objective which most of you will encounter, or have encountered, fairly early in your adult life--planning for a wedding once you have selected and gotten acceptance from a potential spouse. Again, for illustrative purposes, I might mention that some caution might be an appropriate strategy to blend with natural enthusiasm. Please don't argue with the steps/tasks I have used in the illustration--just recognize the goodness of the chart in thorough, comprehensive planning. See Figure 2.

This concludes my lecture-style advice regarding choosing a college and making the most of those enjoyable years. The chapters which follow are largely anecdotal reflecting actual happenings in my life from which I learned valuable lessons which I desire--feel compelled-

-to share with you as you head into your post-college life and careers. If you have learned nothing more from the foregoing chapters, I hope you will retain and use my passionate hope that you will <u>get serious sooner, learn to better know yourself, develop your personal understanding of mission and vision(s), choose wisely, and appreciate the vital importance of thorough planning.</u>

*Figure 2*

GANTT CHART ILLUSTRATION
PLANNING A WEDDING

| Task/Activity | Weeks in Planning for Event (1–25) | Responsibility |
|---|---|---|
| Decide range of wedding dates | weeks 1–3 △ | Bride & Groom |
| Meet with clergy - Schedule church & counseling | weeks 1–3 △ | B & G |
| Find & schedule reception hall | weeks 3–4 △ | B & Parents (B) |
| Attend counseling with pastor | weeks 3–5 △ | B & G |
| Select attendants & notify | weeks 5–8 △ | B & G |
| Design wedding ceremony | weeks 5–8 △ | B & G |
| Select & get wedding rings | weeks 6–9 △ | B & G |
| Decide on attire & procure | weeks 6–14 △ | B & G |
| Arrange musician services | weeks 6–10 △ | B & G |
| Determine invitees | weeks 5–8 △ | B & G |
| Plan reception program & menu | weeks 5–8 △ | B & G |
| Design invitations & procure | weeks 6–11 △ | B & Parents (B) |
| Address & mail invitations | weeks 10–13 △ | B & Parents (B) |
| Schedule rehearsal & notify participants | weeks 6–9 △ | B & G |
| Arrange for post-rehearsal dinner | weeks 13–17 △ | G & Parents (G) |
| Get gifts for attendants | weeks 13–17 △ | B & G |
| Identify wanted gifts & notify selected stores | weeks 6–13 △ | B |
| Engage photographer | weeks 6–9 △ | B & Parents (B) |
| Plan honeymoon & make reservations | weeks 6–20 △ | B & G |
| Rehearsal & dinner | week 21 △ | B, G & Parents (G) |
| Wedding day | week 22 △ | B, G & Parents |
| Pay fees & bills | weeks 22–23 △ | Parents |

# Courtship and Marriage - Some Thoughts from a Realist Who Has Been (and Is) There

Back in the mid-nineties, while still teaching at Taylor University, I would often ask graduating seniors what their plans were for life after college, hoping to get some responses related to career strategies. More often than not, however, their answers were to"get a job (usually nothing specific) and get married". Today, marriage shortly after college graduation is not so much in vogue with both males and females generally preferring to live as singles for longer periods of time before committing to a binding relationship. Regardless of timing, marriage is a very serious issue and should lead to a lifetime of mutual understanding, support, and happiness. I, personally, am a veteran of 56 years of wonderful (with very few exceptions) spousal relationships--29 years with Aileen before her cancer-caused demise, followed by 27 great ongoing years with Jane. This experience has led to development of a few important thoughts--some not likely to be popular with everybody--which I will pass on in this section.

Marriage is a <u>sacred commitment</u>. Indeed, it is one of the seven sacraments observed by the Roman Catholic Church. It is a matter of personal integrity and following biblical principles that wedding promises made during a wedding ceremony not be violated. This argues strongly for not being prematurely caught up by fun and physical impulses. Yes, these elements are important, but it much more vital to answer the question: " Do I really want to spend the rest of my life with this person as my companion, best friend, lover, and mother/father of my children?".

My present pastor, Dr. Ron Naylor, conducted a "picture book" wedding ceremony for my youngest daughter and a fine young man (ages 24 and 25 respectively) who had known each other since high school days. Both were/are bright, attractive, personable, and excellent athletes. Pastor Naylor focused his homily/sermon on the principle that " marriage is not just a sprint. It is a marathon"--a very meaningful message for the bride and groom, their families, and attending friends.

Similarly, another favorite Presbyterian pastor, Rev. Tom Tewell, officiated at the first wedding of my oldest daughter to another fine young man (both in their early twenties) and also blessed with the excellent attributes mentioned above. Pastor Tewell's message followed typical Presbyterian homiletic structure, i.e. three or four points, each beginning with same letter. He said that a sound marriage relationship should be enduring, exemplary, encouraging, and exciting. The last two adjectives deserve some brief fleshing out since failure in these areas contributed to this first relationship not enduring. Happily, my oldest daughter (a skilled professional) and her present husband, a great, high ranking executive of an engineering construction firm--both in their forties--found each other and have a wonderful marriage based on Golden Rule principles.

Regarding the "encouraging" principle: More often than not, in today's society, both husband and wife choose to work outside the home. Sometimes, both parties find themselves pursuing "fast track" careers. In other situations, perhaps just one spouse can anticipate significant career growth; and in still other cases, maybe both husband and wife may be limited to gainful employment which helps to support their family and provide non-vocational opportunities. Of course, family arrangements with stay-at-home moms and/or dads are still not uncommon. Regardless of the family situation, it is vitally important that spouses understand, appreciate, respect and encourage each other in their chosen endeavors--even when some discomfort is involved. Such possibilities should be thoroughly discussed and understood before entering into a commitment intended to last for a lifetime.

The "exciting" principle is also very important. Believe it or not, the initial euphoria attending a wedding will someday diminish-- but true love should expand and deepen, particularly if nourished by giving high priority to doing things together as a couple and showing appreciation for each other. As employment pressures grow and children arrive in the family, it is not uncommon for husbands and wives to take each other for granted. This should not be allowed to happen even though "keeping the bloom on the rose" may require some overt planning and effort. Maintaining physical attractiveness is important as is satisfying sexual desires. Also, remembering special days, e.g. birthdays and anniversaries--and just spur-of-the-moment times--with gifts, flowers, nice dinners out, mutually enjoyable activities (concerts, shows, sporting events, etc.) will help maintain a fun relationship. Beyond that, ongoing genuine interest and communication regarding each partner's interests and activities is vital. Family meals, taken together, should not be given up despite pressures to the contrary. Of course, occasional "second honeymoon" trips can be great fun while rebuilding and further cementing loving relationships. Good marriages can/should be exciting and happy throughout spouses' lifetimes.

Mutually shared spiritual beliefs will help bolster efforts to create and maintain a happy marital relationship. The apostle Paul advises folks to "not be yoked together with unbelievers" (2Corinthians 6:14). Worshipping together and sharing interests and activities in the work of a church will be uplifting and also increase bonding. Not behaving thusly can provoke friction and unhappiness. In my first marriage, Aileen and I enjoyed and benefitted from a number of Lutheran churches as we moved around the country. Then came a time when Aileen responded to an emotional altar call at a fundamentalist church where, after the service, a church elder spoke to us and pointedly said to her, "Well, at least now you're saved", implying that I was not. Consequently, as we attended that church, I was treated as a semi-heathen while Aileen became increasingly interested and involved in questionable fundamentalist teachings and doctrines--all of which led to a period of considerable unhappiness in our marriage. Fortunately, our oldest daughter, Deb, introduced us to New Providence Presbyterian Church in New Jersey where Pastor Tom Tewell preached eloquently from the Bible and made it relevant to daily life. Here Aileen and I found a spiritual home we both could embrace and happiness returned to our marriage, ultimately resulting in our mutual decision to sacrificially accept an opportunity to teach and provide some leadership at Taylor University, a Christian college in central Indiana.

No treatment of courtship and marriage would be complete without a discussion of sex--something many/most readers have eagerly awaited. First, let me assure you that I am not a prude. I am a normal American male who very much appreciates and respects females. However, going through adolescence, young manhood, and even the aging process, I have experienced feelings of lust and arousal--just like most of my male counterparts. Fortunately, though, I have been able to practice abstinence in sexual relationships other than in my two marriages. For this, I give credit to my parental upbringing, increasing efforts to follow biblical teachings, good groups of friends which held each other accountable, and common sense. It's not that I didn't have opportunities and temptations (more about this shortly); but, the rewards stemming from this discipline have been many. First and foremost are the wonderful feelings which attend engaging in physical acts of love with one's wife/husband--feelings far deeper than just satisfying physical lust. Somehow, despite natural desires but perhaps with God's help, I was able to forestall the ultimate in love making with my wives-to-be until our wedding nights--and then, Wow!! Other benefits deriving from abstinence include avoiding: possibilities of creating unplanned, unwanted children; emotional struggles with the temptations of abortion; ongoing feelings of guilt; and acquiring STDs (sexually transmitted diseases).

Spousal love making involves a heavy dose of mutual trust in each other's faithfulness. I am proud and grateful to say that I have never cheated on either of my two wives; but it's not that there haven't been opportunities. You, too, will experience similar temptations and problems unless you elect to live in a monastery. For illustrative purposes, I will describe a few situations I encountered in the following paragraphs.

Long periods of time away from home can weaken personal defenses and make one more susceptible to temptations. During my time in the Navy, I observed this while engaged in a number of lengthy cruises. Prostitutes and their pimps are particularly aware of this natural weakness and see it as an opportunity to prey upon lonely sailors. After about three weeks at sea, our aircraft carrier anchored off of the port city of Naples, Italy. Crew members were awarded one or two days of liberty on shore, and were greeted at the dock by girls and their pimps who said things like "you come see my sister--she virgin". How ridiculous, but not infrequently successful in entrapping both young men and old salts seeking adventure. Many of these guys returned to the ship having been infected with a variety of sexually transmitted diseases. Similarly, a number of the men got drunk and were lured into tattoo parlors where they were " decorated" with questionable, permanent artwork in studios of questionable cleanliness. Many of the guys deeply regretted their foolishness when they returned to sanity, and spent months thereafter using sandpaper trying to remove their tattoos under the advice of a shipboard doctor.

Upon leaving the Navy, I joined the Eastman Kodak Company in Rochester, New York, as an industrial engineer. Kodak was a great company to work for. I learned much, made excellent progress, formed many friendships, and had fun--some of which involved attending many after-hours parties which occured quite frequently to celebrate almost anything. These company oriented get-togethers usually involved eating, drinking, and dancing--and rarely included spouses. This can be dangerous! One very attractive female employee of my department liked to dance very closely with any males who wanted to enjoy her company. I can still picture her on the dance floor with one of my friends, who was married with two young children. The two of them became enamored and my friend divorced his wife in favor of this sensuous female. This unpleasant development caused our department to alter its partying practices in terms of reduced frequency and encouraging involvement of spouses and dates.

There is a message here. Work environments today inevitably present opportunities for men and women to participate and associate with members of the opposite gender--hopefully in productive and respectful relationships. Overnight business trips and lengthy engagments away from home are not uncommon. In business situations, men and women generally look and behave their best. Temptations can arise, and married men and women need to remember their marital commitments. At the same time, spouses staying at home or working in some other employment environment need to continue also looking their best and behaving winsomely when they are with their wives/husbands. Marital excitement must be maintained in order to offset temptations that are bound to occur in the workplace. Such temptations can be even stronger, and human beings more vulnerable, in situations where professional people, e.g. pastors, teachers, medical practitioners, and lawyers, must deal with emotional issues presented by their parishoners, students, patients, and clients.

Fast forward in your imaginations now to a time when I was forty years old and was taken on an overnight business trip, to Baltimore, by my boss--a senior executive fifteen years older than I. My boss was a very impressive individual who really knew his way around, albeit being married to a fine, attractive lady. After dinner, John insisted that we visit a lounge with which he was familiar, and so we went to this relatively fancy place which I soon began to view as an "upholstered sewer". Once inside, John busied himself flirting with a number of unattached females with whom he seemed familiar. Left by myself, I found a barstool in a corner and tried to nurse one beer through the remainder of the evening. Soon, a hard-looking but attractive female, in high heels and a low-cut blouse, sat down beside me and began to talk. She asked me to buy her a drink and, trying to behave like a gentleman, I complied with her request. Subsequently, she downed four more drinks, which looked like manhattans but were actually tea--all charged to my tab/bill. I learned later that this female was a bar girl whose job it was to get lounge patrons to ring up big bar bills while she, simultaneously, tried to sell herself. She rubbed her leg against mine and giggled while some other lounge females performed acts which would make the producers of <u>Playboy</u> magazine blush. Things got to a point where I could take it no longer. I excused myself, found John, and told him I felt uncomfortable and would take a taxi back to the hotel. We parted company, and I found my way back to my room where I experienced feelings of anger for having allowed myself to be lured into that "sewer", and shame for not having extricated myself much sooner. My displeasure and departure did not hurt my relationship with my boss, and I think he actually respected me for my beliefs and behavior. However, I was happy to be transferred to another location shortly after this episode.

I repeat, I have never cheated on my wife. However, my biggest temptation came at age 44 and partly includes the unequal yoking problems discussed earlier in this chapter. The following situation might be described by saying that flirting can be fun--but dangerous.

It began when I was facilitating a week long seminar on productivity improvement in Philadelphia. One of my students was a facility manager named Diane (fictitious name). She was in her early forties and very attractive. When I dismissed the group for lunch during the first day, Diane delayed her departure and asked me to join her for lunch. We ate quickly and returned well before the end of the ninety minutes allowed for lunch. However, during that break time she shared a domestic problem caused by her being a lifetime mainline Christian, and now being badgered by her husband who had recently become heavily involved in a radical fundamentalist group and was wanting-- almost demanding--that she convert to the same radical doctrines.

This struck a responsive chord with me since I was experiencing similar, albeit not so extreme, problems in my marriage. Consequently, we ate lunch together during the remaining four days of the seminar, and shared some rather deep discussions of common interests and problems. At the end of the seminar, I said goodbye to the participants and, again, Diane stayed until last and told me that she could stay in Philadelphia that night. I thought nothing of this, but told her to call me if she was ever again in Philadelphia.

She did have business in Philadelphia twice during the ensuing year, and she did call me, and we did have lunch together both times. At the end of the second lunch visit, Diane said,"you know, this is almost like having an affair". Again, I shrugged this off and went back to work.

About six months later, I was working on a lengthy consulting assignment in Harrisburg, Pennsylvania, and was staying, during the work weeks, at a nice resort/motel at the edge of the city. One day, shortly after leaving work, I took a dip in the motel's outdoor swimming pool and guess who was there--Diane, on a business trip and looking very attractive in a decent swim suit. We renewed acquaintanceship, talking in the jacuzzi, and arranged to have dinner together at a restaurant known for superb Beef Wellington.

Returning to the motel, Diane invited me into her room where we talked some more. I got up to leave and, at the door, gave Diane a hug--perhaps a bit closer than I should have --whereupon she kissed me and asked me to stay with her overnight (using language more descriptive than is appropriate in this book). I declined and left.

About 2:00 AM, the phone in my room awakened me from a sound sleep. It was Diane, calling to tell me that she couldn't get to sleep and would I please come back and keep her company. Again, I declined--somewhat grumpily.

The next morning, I saw Diane in the motel lobby and she wouldn't speak to me. Someone once said, "Hell hath no wrath like a woman scorned". Thus ended my friendship/relationship with Diane. Again, I was and am grateful for having been blessed with Christian teachings and a strong sense of marital commitment and integrity which enabled me to withstand a very real temptation. I don't know how I could have faced my wife and children if I had yielded. The Bible says, in 1 Corinthians 10:13 that: "God is faithful; he will not let you be tempted beyond what you can bear. But, when you are tempted, he will also provide a way out so you can stand up under it."

Before leaving this chapter, filled with relatively risque illustrations of temptations, let me emphasize the importance of committed fidelity in marriage. Among the many standards set forth by my church (Presbyterian) is that pastors and church officers must live either in fidelity within the covenant of marriage between a man and a woman, or chastity in singleness. This is a good rule, not only for church officials, but also for people in general. Infidelity often leads to divorce, and I have seen, many times, the pain which attends dissolving a marriage--trauma for the divorcing parties both during and after the legal procedures--and also for the children of the parents who are terminating their family. Marriage can and should be a wonderful relationship; and it is very important to prepare carefully, and then do it and maintain it, harmoniously, the first time.

Finally, I want it known that I have enjoyed two wonderful marriages, spanning 56 years at this writing. The only "downer" was the brief period in my first marriage which was caused by religious differences exacerbated by fundamentalist dogmatism. Fortunately, this was resolved. However, it left me with a need to warn couples, who plan to marry, that spirituality is an important element in human beings; and it is wise to avoid unequal spiritual yoking or determine to live with, and respect, spouses religious differences. Both of my marriages have been harmonious, and especially my second marriage wherein Jane and I live by the Golden Rule in our relationships with each other despite not always wanting the same things. May this be so with you and your families.

# Shortly After Graduation From College

**Don't indulge in excessive idle time after graduation or between jobs.**

Do something constructive even if it is not in line with your career path desires and plans. Long time voids in a resume will be questioned by prospective employers--thinking that this might indicate a lack of high ambition.

Yes, you probably deserve a short vacation after a long educational grind, but, even then, it might be something constructive like a trip to one or more foreign countries. Also, job opportunities might be tight at graduation time, but you can seek temporary employment or become responsibly involved in volunteer charitable work, some of which can offer a basic stipend, e.g. Americorps, Peace Corps, Habitat for Humanity, etc..

As you approach graduation (during your senior year) and throughout your entire career, don't hesitate to aggressively make use of the career development organization at your college or university. You will have paid dearly to obtain a quality education, and a good quality school should offer sound career guidance, attract a sizeable number of employers to recruit on campus, and maintain an active and effective alumni networking system. As a prospective employee, searching for appropriate opportunities, the career development office at your alma mater could be a valuable source of contacts with whom you have a common interest. Similarly, later in your career, as an employer looking for top quality candidates for employment, the alumni career office should be a very viable source in which to search.

Many books are available offering advice regarding career planning and job search. Make use of one or more of them. Specifically, I can recommend <u>What Color is Your Parachute?, a Practical Manual for Job Seekers and Career Changers</u> by Richard Nelson Bolles. This easily read book, which is regularly updated, will help you better understand who you are, what you want to do, and where you want to do it--then, provide helpful advice regarding how to find and pursue opportunities which match your aspirations.

If you are unsure, at graduation time, of where you should be heading in life, or if your college training is not currently in demand, you might consider spending some time in the military services. Ideally, this would mean gaining acceptance into an Officers' Candidate School, provided by most of the services (Army, Navy, and Coast Guard), graduating as a commissioned officer, and then serving an obligatory tour of duty before returning to civilian life--or, perhaps deciding to make a full career of military service. In my own life, I was prompted, by the Korean Conflict, to go through Navy OCS at Newport, Rhode Island, and then serve three years as a commissioned aircraft maintenance officer--this, despite having offers at graduation time to be employed as an industrial engineer at three prestigious companies. OCS was tough, but I will be forever grateful for my service time wherein I gained more maturity and learned management and leadership skills, all of which made me very employable upon my release from active duty. My oldest son experienced similar benefits from Coast Guard OCS, albeit not in wartime, but allowing him time for additional maturation and overcoming having earned a degree for which their was little employment demand.

## Develop contacts which can lead to referrals and favorable reference letters.

Such networking can begin during high school years and continue throughout your lifetime. <u>Many</u> employment opportunities are found as a result of a respected friend asking an employer to be willing to receive your resume and grant a brief interview. That is really all you should expect from a contact (not an automatic job offer), but, if given an opportunity to sell yourself, it's then up to you to do so.

Favorable networking contacts may come from relatives; but, more often for most of us, they result from prior employment and constructive involvement in community activities and charitable endeavors sponsored by churches and similar organizations. Of course, one's primary goals in such extra-curricular and/or non-job-related work should be to serve others--not self-grandiosity. The beneficial relationships just develop naturally.

## Corporate Culture is Very Important.

Consider corporate culture carefully when considering and pursuing employment by any organization you intend to spend much time with--perhaps an entire career. Will you be proud to be a part of this company, governmental group, or non-profit organization? What do they do, and how do they do it? E.g. Would you enjoy marketing tobacco products to third world countries or writing articles for tabloid magazines, or working for a company whose Chief Executive Officer is nicknamed "Chainsaw"? Less drastic examples are firms whose products and services are of questionable quality, where lower level employees are considered merely "factors of production", and where unethical and immoral behavior is common practice.

If possible, seek and find an organization led by a top executive you can respect and believe in--with a sound, noble, respected mission and exciting vision(s)--embracing all stakeholders and not just profit. (Stakeholders include customers, employees, owners/stockholders, suppliers, and the community.)

I, personally, experienced a "roller coaster" career relative to corporate culture. I started at the top with the Eastman Kodak Company during its heyday of manufacturing and processing film, making high quality cameras, and pioneering work on copiers and military optics. I was enjoying a "fast track" career development program, but was drawn away by an impatient quest for higher position and more pay. This resulted in moves to a large chemical company, a smaller plastics firm, and, at the very bottom of my career (culture-wise) a small family-owned confectionery company. Each job change was accompanied by increased compensation and more responsibility--but, also increased unhappiness due to worsening corporate culture. Fortunately, I was able to recover from the cultural "pits" in which I found myself. On the way back up, I served as plant manager, and then general manager for another large chemical company, and finally landed back on top with two outstanding employers, from a corporate culture standpoint,--Price Waterhouse and Taylor University.

I learned, the hard way, about the importance of corporate culture, and I am hoping that you readers will be wiser than I was earlier in your careers.

## Leave an Employer Graciously if You Must Leave

Don't burn bridges behind you when it becomes time to leave an employer. You may have justifiable (even negative) reasons for departing, but it is always wise to leave on a high note--giving ample notice and not being negatively critical of your superiors and organization (except perhaps in a private, constructive discussion with your immediate supervisor). Said differently, you need to leave a favorable impression with the employer from which you are departing. You should want to be able to use that employer as a reference in your quest for future job changes, and you will want that person(s) to describe you in favorable terms. Prior employers may find themselves in legal jeopardy if they "bad mouth" an ex-employee during a reference check, so they will often restrict their reference discussions to confirming the time and position of employment. However, if you have left with a good record and under positive circumstances, many prior employers will be pleased to share this information. In other words, a job candidate can be damned by faint praise or no praise at all.

## Prepare Thoroughly for Contacts with Prospective Employers

Develop and display knowledge of each potential emplorer, starting with initial correspondence and continuing throughout the entire interview and selection process. John F. Kennedy is often quoted as saying," Ask not what your country can do for you. Instead, ask what you can do for your country." This certainly applies to your relationships with a future employer. Instead of concentrating on compensation and fringe benefits, inquire as to how you can quickly become a significant contributing factor in the organization, and what sort of career path progression could you work toward based on earned achievements and, perhaps, continued education. Discussions regarding future, company-related objectives and responsibilities will be viewed much more favorably than flaunting past honors and achievements.

## Understand Other People, Respect Them (In Most Cases), and Honor Their Dignity

Most readers of this book will have, like I have, grown up in relatively priviliged circumstances--good families, good schools, good communities, good colleges, and good churches or other religious organizations. It is quite easy to ignore less fortunate situations from which many people come, making up a large segment of the American work force and voting public. It is very important, and only right, that folks understand and respect each other in terms of their backgrounds, cultures, skills, beliefs and aspirations--and, above all, do nothing to denigrate or destroy another persons dignity. Shortly after graduating from college, many of you will be employed in supervisory positions wherein you are responsible for people with less education and/or ambition, but who have been working for many years, gaining much knowledge and experience, from whom you can learn if you treat them with understanding and respect.

Immediately after graduating from Drexel University, Navy Officer Candidate School, Aircraft Ground Officers' School, and Aircraft Engine and Structural Maintenance School, I was assigned to an air/anti submarine squadron operating out of the Naval Base in Norfolk, Virginia. Here, I was to serve three years as Assistant Maintenance Officer, supervising approximately fifty enlisted men, led by six chief petty officers, in the scheduling, servicing, and maintenance of approximately twenty AF Guardian airplanes (subsequently replaced by S2F Sentinels). The mission of this squadron was to be prepared to find and destroy enemy submarines if such ever became necessary. As a twenty three year old ensign, fresh out of college and Navy schools, I was awestruck by this responsibility. All of a sudden, men who had as much as twenty five years experience in the Navy, were required to salute me and I was expected to answer to my superiors for their performance as my squadron pursued an "E for Excellence" award. Initially, I felt somewhat like Lieutenant Fuzz, the newly commissioned officer in the Beetle Bailey Comic Strip.

Fortunately, I was able to quickly earn the respect and cooperation of the chief petty officers and other non-commissioned officers in my squadron by admitting my inexperience along with my eagerness to support them as a team as we strove to meet and surpass the expectations of our commanding officer. I remember, with great fondness and respect,

Chief Petty Officers Benjamin and Phillips who were outstanding mentors for me as I matured in my responsible position.

The basic truth incorporated in this story is that leaders at all levels, and in any field, will do well to surround themselves with people (subordinates and peers), who know more than they do, who are willing and proud to share their knowledge and experience, and whom you can trust as a member of a team pursuing known visions and objectives. Of course, team members must understand and respect the fact that the leader is responsible for making decisions based on input from his/her team coupled with his/her wisdom and awareness of expectations from his/her superiors or constituencies.

People in subordinate positions are sometimes/often in need of support from their immediate superiors. I am reminded, with pride, of a situation involving one of my older chief petty officers. Our squadron was in the final phases of a continuous 48 hour operation, aboard an aircraft carrier, simulating war combat conditions. One of our aircraft, being readied for catapult launch, was found to have a flat tire. The Air Boss, a commander rank in charge of this training exercise, got extremely ticked off and ordered my maintenance chief on the hangar deck to personally carry a replacement tire (big and very heavy) up to the flight deck and supervise its installation. The elderly chief replied that he couldn't and wouldn't do this, and for this the Air Boss listed the chief for disciplinary action in the form of a captain's mast (lower than a court martial). As Assistant Maintenance Officer, I was to be a witness at the captain's mast hearing. I proceded to defend the chief in terms of fatigue, outstanding performance throughout the exercise, and the possibility of physical harm if the chief attempted to carry the tire up the ladder from the hangar deck to the flight deck deck. I then accepted responsibility for the flat tire. The case against the chief was dismissed, and I gained many points from my crew.

## Join and Participate in Professional and Civic Organizations

Continued learning should be a lifetime occupation for people in all occupations. Once you have landed a job and know what you are to do and where you are to live, it is not sufficient, career-wise, to merely satisfy the requirements of your new position. Professionally, there are certifications to be earned and organizations to be joined. Also, graduate programs and degrees may be not only desirable--but indeed necessary--to continue employment and make significant progress in many occupational fields.

Professional organizations help members keep up to date in changing developments in their respective fields; and <u>things do change!</u> In my field of management, many new philosophies, programs and practices have emerged during my 45(+) year career. Some were faddish and have been forgotten, while many have continuing value and need to be in a successful manager's tool kit. A representative few of these are: Time Management, Work Simplification, Value Analysis, project planning via Gantt Charts, Manufacturing Resource Planning (MRP), Total Quality Management (TQM), Break Even Analysis, Supply Chain Management, Return on Investment and Net Present Value, empowerment leadership, teamwork training and practice, Lean, Six Sigma, etc. It is vital that managers and practitioners stay current with developments in their field(s). Professional associations help via regularly scheduled meetings, publications, and conferences. In my career, I gained much from belonging to organizations related to management, industrial engineering, the plastics industry, and management consulting. Sadly, I did not do much to maintain a "cutting edge" knowledge of computerized data processing and information systems as its rapid emergence has changed our lives and world. I allowed myself to become so busy with my management responsibilities and creative ideas that I neglected to take advantage of training opportunities in digital technology as they became available. Consequently, at this writing, I am semi-obsolete in modern information technology--an uncomfortable feeling. All this is to say: Do continue your learning process throughout your entire life, even into retirement. This will require discipline and dedication, but it will pay dividends--both in professional growth and self esteem and happiness.

Active participation and leadership in professional organizations can do much more than feed you with needed information. Meeting people with similar interests from other providers of goods and services, and other geographical areas, can/will give opportunities to share experiences and ideas, build a broad-based reputation, establish valuable contacts, and make good friends. Involvement in local chapter meetings and attendance at national/international conferences are particularly helpful in expanding your knowledge and visions.

Your life should/will have many facets; faith, family, work/ profession, and civic interests and responsibilities. Regarding the latter, you will do well to become involved in the community in which you live--even as a young newcomer. Many towns and cities sponsor and conduct, for a modest fee, "Academies for Community Leadership" wherein citizens (mostly younger) learn about community history, politics, government, local agencies and organizations, strengths, and weaknesses. Such courses normally run about thirteen weeks and provide excellent networking opportunities. As you become more familiar with your home surroundings and earn some recognition, you might consider joining a civic service organization such as Rotary, Kiwanis, Lions, Exchange, etc. Here you will find increased opportunities to serve locally, nationally, and/or worldwide--and also make good friends and valuable contacts, enjoy good programs and fellowship, and have fun.

## Regarding Graduate Schools:

When considering a graduate school/program, <u>choose a good one.</u> Grad programs abound, but employers do know the difference between those at the top, mid-level schools, and "diploma mills" at the bottom. Better schools attract better students, thereby causing better learning from fellow students. This also leads to providing better networking contacts throughout your career. Many grad school students have said that they learn as much or more from fellow students as from the professors. Grad school is another big investment in time and money. Do choose wisely. School reputations are quite widely known, and many rating systems are published in the media.

## Know What's Going On In Your World

Time is a precious asset in your life; but, once each minute, hour, day is passed, it is gone forever. Therefore, it is very important to use time wisely! Granted, cell phone chatter and texting can be fun, as can be many other activities such as reading gossip magazines and watching lightweight shows such as "American Idol", reality shows, "Desperate Housewives", etc.. However, it might be well to challenge yourself with the question:"Is this the best use of my time right now?"

Now, I am not against relaxing and having fun, and indeed it is important for folks to be conversant about current movies, shows, sporting events, etc. at social gatherings. However, for your own career growth and how you appear to others (peers, superiors, and lower level asociates) it is even more important that you discipline yourself to keep abreast of current news, using at least four sources to provide coverage of local doings, national and worldwide news, and events and developments pertaining to your profession/occupation, e.g. business, medicine, hospitality, retailing, etc. Unfortunately, recent technology and economic conditions have caused local and regional newspapers to shrink in size and concentrate mostly on local issues, e.g. crime, politics, social doings, and gossip; but, if you are going to function well as a citizen, you need to know about things that are going on where you live and how best to accept and/or deal with them. Beyond that, there are credible national newspapers and magazines, news coverage on TV and internet, professional journals, and books(yes, books!). In my view, no American citizen should be unaware of the content in Thomas L. Friedman's two recent books, <u>The World is Flat</u> and <u>Hot, Flat and Crowded</u>.

Book-wise, national newspapers and bookstores publish up-to-date listings of the most popular books; fiction, non-fiction, and (in my field,) business. Many summary services are available to help readers capture the essence of chosen books without reading the whole volume. Again, in my field of business, I am fond of a service called <u>Executive Summaries</u> which provides, for an annual fee of about $150, two five page summaries each month capturing the important content of two current and widely read business books. These summaries can be shared with friends and associates.

## Personal Finance Issues

Live within your means!! Credit cards are a "bummer" unless you use them primarily for convenience and pay off whatever you owe at the end of each monthly billing cycle. Countless young people have used credit cards--perhaps many of them--to satisfy desires for instant materialistic gratification, resulting in creation of large debts which they are unable to pay while creditor organizations are charging exploitative interest on unpaid balances. As I write this, American society is suffering through the worst recession experienced since the "Great Depression" in the early 1930s. To a large extent, this was caused by greedy financial organizations and unworthy borrowers of money making unwise use of poorly structured credit opportunities. Granted, credit has been, and is, a vital ingredient in our country's economic growth; however, borrowers should be convinced of their ability to pay their debt obligations on time, and creditor institutions must be even more convinced of their clients' ability to pay off what they owe. Of course, there must be opportunities for financiers, e.g. venture capitalists, to fund risky endeavors while charging much higher interest rates to offset the dangers of loss. These foregoing comments pertain to individuals and families as well as corporations and other organizations.

An excellent example of prudent personal finance can be seen in my 96 year old father-in-law, LaVerne LeMaster. This gentleman, from northern Indiana, never attended college or enjoyed a high-level position during his years of employment. However, while working on farms and in factories, he taught himself to become a skilled millwright and then worked as such for a furniture manufacturing company. During this time, he and his wife lived frugally, but still lived well--owning a sequence of comfortable homes and putting their daughter through college--all the while paying their debts and saving for retirement. Consequently, now in widowed retirement, LaVerne is living comfortably in a comprehensive care retirement community which is known as the best in East Central Indiana--and paying his bills from social security and interest earned on his savings. This is a man who has lived through the Great Depression, has been a good family provider and productive employee and community citizen, has lived frugally but well, and has not succumbed to the lures of instant gratification fed by unwise use of credit.

Basic to living within your means and saving something toward emergencies, retirement, and childrens' educations is creation and adherence to a simple budget which includes a cash flow projection. Budgeting is quite easy if you just do it. You must know how much money you will receive each month--when and from what sources-- during a twelve month period. You must also know how much you will be required to spend to satisfy a variety of needs during each month. Monthly receipts and expenditures will not be the same for every month; and here is where a twelve month cash flow projection is valuable.. In terms of income, you might anticipate some quarterly interest/dividend payments from investments, income tax refunds, gifts from relatives at expected times, etc. Expenditure-wise, think of such things as tuition payments, down payment on a car, insurance premiums, fees for recreation, etc.

Cash flow projection forms are widely available, but you easily can make your own. Using a columnar spread sheet (paper or computerized), devote the left-hand column to describe anticipated elements of income and expense. Then use the next thirteen columns for the twelve months of the year and the last column for expected yearly totals for each element. At the top of the sheet, for the first month, enter the cash/liquid amount you will start the month with. Under that, devote a section to listing the different sources and amounts of expected income. Add the various incomes and then add this total to your starting balance. This tells you how much money you have to use during the month. Then, in the next section in the first month's column, under the incomes listing, enter your planned expense items (some regular monthly and some due less frquently). Add the monthly expenses and subtract this total from what is expected to be available. If this result (difference) is positive--hopefully so--this will become your starting balance for the next month, and you continue this exercise for the next eleven months of the year. Negative anticipated results (differences) at the end of any month will indicate that your planned expenditures will exceed your available resources, and you will need to do something about this--cut costs, add income, or borrow money--or maybe all of the above. Hopefully, a borrowing solution will be utilized only if really necessary, and then envision a relatively short term payback period.

Using such a cash flow analysis as part of your budget will help immensely in your planning process and will minimize unpleasant surprises.

Begin saving for retirement and childrens' education as a part of your budget as soon as possible. Also, don't forget obligations to the Lord, His church, and related activities and charities. If tithing is impossible early on, at least remember God with proportionate giving, i.e. some percentage of income taken from the top, not just what's left over after paying all other expenses.

Finally, no matter what your occupation is, please be aware of the advantages of compound interest in your plans to save money for future purposes. Allowing interest to compound means not withdrawing the interest earned by your investments (savings accounts, certficates of deposit, bonds, stock, etc.) but rather allowing the interest and dividends to accumulate within your investment portfolio which then grows and should normally earn an even larger amount of interest/ dividends in the next year, and ensuing years. The mathematical formula representing this important facet of saving is;

$$F = P \ (1 + i)^n, \text{ where:}$$

$$F = \text{Future Value}$$
$$P = \text{Present Value}$$
$$i = \text{Interest Rate (Annual)}$$
$$n = \text{Number of Years Invested}$$

An interesting and helpful relationship dealing with compound interest is known as "The Rule of 72". If you divide 72 by any interest rate, you will learn the number of years it will take for an investment to double in value, assuming interest is allowed to compound with no withdrawals. Similarly, if you want to invest in a way that your money will double in "X" number of years--assuming interest is allowed to compound with no withdrawals--divide 72 by "X" years and you will learn the interest rate which must be found for your investment to achieve this doubling objective. To illustrate, imagine that a 22 year old person manages to save $2,000 in his/her first year of full-time employment, and invests it at an annual percentage yield of 6.0%, with interest compounding. Following "The Rule of 72", this investment will double, to $4,000, in twelve years, by which time the person will be 34 years old. It will double again to $8,000 by age 46; double again to $16,000 by age 58; and double again to $32,000 by retirement at age 70. Now, imagine how much this person would accumulate by retirement time if he/she saved just $2,000 every year and allowed the compound interest to build the investment. Similarly, following the "Rule of 72", if you can find an interest rate of 8%, your investment fund will double every nine years, and you will accumulate $64,000 by age 67--all from an initial investment of $2,000 at age 22.

## Learn to Play Golf

It was not until I was forty years old that I learned how important it can be, if one is mingling with professional and managerial types of people, to play golf reasonably well--or at least be reasonably conversant in the subject and feel at home in a country club setting. During my early career years, I worked hard and well. Otherwise, I busied myself with family, church and community activities; along with, for recreation: gardening, woodworking, tennis, and playing softball. I played a grand total of nine holes of golf on a nearby course during all of that time.

Then, shortly after joining the professional firm of Price Waterhouse & Co., I was invited/expected to attend and participate in my home office's annual golf outing at a prestigious, suburban country club. So, I borrowed a set of clubs and was assigned to a foursome. Approaching the first tee, I noticed a small group of senior partners of the firm standing around watching the action. Scared of making a fool of myself, I prayed, "Lord, please let me at least hit the ball, and reasonably straight". I was guilty of wrongfully using a baseball-type swing, but I did hit the ball and escaped the partners' surveillance. I subsequently learned how so many relationships--business and social--are formed on the golf links, and I tried with only modest success to catch up . Golf actually is fun, and I urge you to add this lifetime sport to your "bag of tricks".

# Anecdotal Lessons Applicable Throughout Career

**(In no particular order)**

**Take the High Road--Hold to what is ethical and right, while simultaneously achieving success and respect. Be a regular guy/gal within self-imposed limits without being prudish--thereby <u>earning the right to be heard.</u>**

During my four months at Navy Officer Candidate School in Newport, Rhode Island, shortly after graduating from college, I was fortunate to gain respect and friendship by virtue of academic success and athletic ability. I was not subjected to much temptation since our free (liberty) time was very limited, and I spent most of this time traveling to New York City to visit my bride who came up from Philadelphia to see me. After graduation from OCS, my wife and I spent the next 24 weeks at two training stations, and here we enjoyed the company and friendship of numerous newly minted junior officers and their wives.

Then, it was time to begin doing some real work, and I was assigned to an air-anti-submarine squadron based on the east coast; and I began to be exposed to some of the seamier sides of life and the temptations that go with it. I learned to accompany friends and associates to beer parties and after-work gatherings, enjoying their company while carefully avoiding anything remotely approaching "tipsiness" or intoxication. I also refused to go to shows and events which promised to be really raunchy. This pattern continued until I joined Taylor University, at age 50, and embraced their behavioral standards which prohibited alcoholic beverages, tobacco, drugs, and immoral conduct.

One regretable exception to this personal policy of mine, prior to employment by Taylor, was when I accompanied my boss to the "upholstered sewer" described earlier in this book. Interestingly, our client in this assignment was the owner of a liquor distributorship which was experiencing significant losses of expensive bottled liquor from his warehouse inventory. After a short investigation, we found that the losses were attributable to one warehouse employee who wore an overcoat to work whenever the weather was the least bit chilly. On these days, he would carry two bottles out of the warehouse using a long cord draped around the back of his neck and tied to the necks of the bottles which were then hidden in the sleeves of the overcoat he was wearing.

While working in "blue collar" manufacturing environments, in positions of increasing responsibility, at Hercules, Polymer, and Thiokol, I gained a respected reputation for making sound decisions, being firm but fair, and being genuinely concerned about the well-being of people working in my areas of responsibilty. I developed friendly relationships with associates and learned about their families, interests, ambitions, and problems. However, I did not indulge in profanity or vulgarity, and, in a short period of time, the incidence of bad language in the plants decreased substantially. Here were cases of subordinate employees and associates copying the behavioral style of a respected leader and fellow employee. It is very important that Christian people, who are blessed with responsible positions, set good behavioral examples as well as performing their managerial and professional duties well.

To illustrate the principle of "earning the right to be heard", I am going to tell a story about a very bright, pesonable young man who graduated from Taylor University three months before I began teaching there, and who became a very good friend during ensuing years. Brian was good enough to be accepted into the MBA (Masters in Business Administration) program at the highly respected Wharton School of the University of Pennsylvania where he performed very well while setting a good moral and ethical example for his friends and classmates. Upon graduation from Wharton, he was employed as a staff consultant, specializing in computerized information systems, in the Management Consulting Division of Arthur Anderson & Co., one of the largest and most highly respected consulting firms in the world.

Six months later, Brian learned of a desperate systems need experienced by a Christian bookship called The Doulos, for which they were unable to pay traditional consulting fees. The Doulos moved from port to port in the "third world", providing publications and some training for folks who wanted to improve their lives. In so doing, the Doulos needed a basic, but sound, inventory control system and a means of better understanding book popularity and usage patterns among folks who patronized the ship's offerings. Brian felt "called" to provide the needed help in systems design and implementation, and asked his new employer, Arthur Anderson, for a leave of absence to do this--a very unusual request for a six-month employee to make. Nevertheless, Arthur Anderson granted the request, and Brian embarked on the Doulos, cruised on this non-luxury ship to many "third world" ports, and completed the installation of the needed systems.

Returning to Arthur Anderson, Brian resumed a successful career path within the firm, and was the subject of an article, describing his Doulos project, which was published in an Arthur Anderson house organ distributed throughout the worldwide organization. Here is an example of an outstanding Christian witness, and "earning the right to be heard".

**Be willing, able, and eager to share your faith--come out of the "closet", but avoid being obnoxious**

Knowing what you believe is very important for your own personal peace of mind and guidance through life. Many/most readers of this book will have had the advantage of growing up in a Christian environment (family and church). It is not unusual, however, for many young adults to experience periods of doubt and indifference to matters of religious faith. The secular world is full of temptations for young people to adopt self-sufficiency attitudes aptly described in the famous poem, Invictus, "I am the master of my fate. I am the captain of my soul". Hopefully, this approach to life will not grossly influence you; but, if it does, please accept my advice to search, with a positive attitude, for a spiritual faith which will sustain you throughout your earthly life and usher you into eternal life. The stakes are huge. This is not something to shrug off, postpone, or purposely ignore.

Many sources are available to help you bolster your Christian beliefs, starting with enlightened study of the Bible, preferably under the tutelage of well-trained and understanding pastors while simultaneously being strengthened by discussions with fellow searchers and believers. Certainly, there are some very basic theological beliefs which all Christians embrace, e.g. accepting Jesus Christ as your savior, based on His teachings, crucifixion, resurrection, and promise of eternal life. However, many doctrinal differences exist among the various church oganizations which have chosen to interpret different passages of scripture in different ways. To my mind, these doctrinal differences are matters of preference and do not represent departures from the basic Christian faith. My Presbyterian pastor, the Rev. Dr. Ronald Naylor, coined a tagline for our congregation, calling for us to embrace "generous orthodoxy". By this, I think he means that we (his parishoners) should hold firm to the basic tenets of the Christian faith, while being respectful, understanding, and tolerant of varied doctrinal practices and beliefs in other Christian organizations.

With a sound, well-informed faith of your own and a "generous orthodoxy attitude", you can be well prepared for winsome witnessing. Different people respond in different ways to various methods of attempting to share our faith. Whole books have been written on the subject of evangelism and it is not my intent to delve deeply into this subject. Admittedly, direct confrontation and distribution of tracts is successful in some cases, as is provision of Christian-oriented shelter, assistance, and training for destitute folks. Such methods are often the purview of folks engaged full-time in missionary activities or perhaps a short-term, church-sponsored missionary project. However, many (perhaps most) readers of this book will spend most of their working lives in secular endeavors related to their profession or some type of management. Too many of these men and women, dedicated believers and churchgoers, feel embarrassed to openly identify themselves as Christians and willingly discuss and share their faith. This is unfortunate. Let me suggest a few basic principles.

- Do your best and be good at some aspects of whatever you do. Earn respect and the opportunity to be copied and/or heard. This applies to folks in all walks of life. I admire the skills and attitudes of all the cashiers, clerks and managers at the food store where my wife and I shop. The same can be said of the Nordstrom chain of department stores. Our appliance repairman has outstanding ability to diagnose, describe, and correct problems. Our family attorney is very knowledgeable, understanding, helpful, and highly ethical. The college president for whom I worked is an outstanding scholar and speaker, while remaining a humble, helpful, servant leader. Many athletes, with whom I have participated, play well, hard, and fair. Such people, and many more, have influenced, by words and deeds, my thoughts, actions, and lifestyle in a variety of ways. When they speak, I listen. Hopefully, I am viewed in a similar manner by my extended family, friends, and associates at all levels.

- As a prelude to sharing your faith, it is very important to develop the skill of listening and building relationships. Listening can be one of the most effective ministries you can offer. The famous American psychologist, Abraham Maslow, identified five sequential human needs, i.e. survival, security, love and belonging, esteem, and self-actualization; each need assuming a primary importance after the prior needs have been satisfied. Listening, empathy, and relationships equate to love and belonging, and it is at that need level that readers of this book can usually be most effective in sharing their faith during their everyday lives. Granted, meeting survival and security needs is very important in dealing with people less fortunate than those who are college bound or college graduates, and this also provides opportunities for sharing faith which are less difficult, but less frequent for most of us.

- If we are good at what we do; and are friendly, helpful, and humble, is there any reason why we should not be willing to openly, yet sensitively, give credit to the God who helped us be what we are? Identifying ourselves as Christians can be done in many tasteful ways, e.g. regular attendance and participation in Christian worship and related activities such as Habitat for Humanity, wearing Christian jewelry (male and female), displaying Christian literature we may be using, quoting scripture passages when truly appropriate, praying at mealtimes and offering prayers at gatherings when invited to do so, etc. For example, a tough but highly respected senior partner (Roman Catholic) in the firm for which I worked kept a Bible on the top of his desk. Tony Dungy, who recently retired as head coach of the Indianapolis Colts, openly tells of his Christian faith throughout his outstanding career as a coach and family man, well described in his book, <u>Quiet Strength</u>. Tim Tebow, great quarterback for the University of Florida, led his team to the national championship, wearing black eye patches inscribed "John 3:16" in the final game of the 2008 season.

- We will encounter many opportunities to be winsome witnesses during our lifetimes. Hopefully, we will exercise the foregoing characteristics, not bludgeoning associates with our beliefs, but being understanding, respectful, sensitive, and helpful as we befriend folks who can be helped by experiencing the "love and belonging" comfort and assurance offered by Jesus Christ. As a final example, I will offer a personal experience. Three years ago, to correct a nasty arythmia condition (irregular and rapid heartbeat), I was subjected to a difficult and somewhat dangerous medical procedure called "catheter ablation". It was successful, and after one night in the hospital, I was preparing to be discharged and leave for home. My surgeon doctor came to my room to check me out, and at the end of his brief examination, I asked him a basic question: " Well, Doctor, now that I'm fixed, how should I live?" I was anticipating an answer dealing with weight loss and exercise. Instead, Doctor Miller said," Do justice, love kindness, and walk humbly with your God" (Micah 6:8). What a wonderful response from a highly skilled Christian physician--whom I had not known to be a Christian.

- On the other hand, I am aware of a situation wherein a group of young people from a conservative Christian college were given an opportunity to visit a number of places of worship, reflecting faiths other than their own, in the Chicago area. The Chicago Loop Synagogue was one such tour stop; and here the rabbi graciously took time to describe the important elements of their sanctuary and explain the basic tenets of the Jewish faith. Two of the students, coming from very fundamentalist backgrounds, then stood and tried to convert the rabbi to Christianity in his own synagogue, challenging his unwillingness to accept Jesus Christ as the Messiah. This was not a good thing to do, and caused much embarrassment for the group and the college being hosted.

- Many of you, circulating with friends and associates who are agnostic or atheistic, may find yourselves engaged in intellectual discussions about religion. Is God real or not? Such a topic was generally shunned in polite society decades ago, but is more commonplace today. Here, as my approach in appropriate situations--embracing cold, hard logic--I like to bring up an adaptation of Pascal's Wager, developed by the highly respected French scientist (hydraulics) and philosopher, Blaise Pascal (living in the 17th century). He reasoned that, although the existence of God can not be proven with absolute scientific certainty, people would be wise to "bet" that God does exist because they have everything to gain and nothing to lose. My adaptation includes accepting Jesus Christ as my savior, enjoying "the gains" of His kingdom here on earth, and anticipating eternal life when I die. Hopefully, such "hard-nosed" logic might cause some skeptics, whose minds are even slightly open, to listen with a more positive, searching attitude to what the Christian faith has to offer. For the open-minded, intellectual seeker, C.S. Lewis' book, Mere Christianity is highly recommended.

## Problem Solving and Decision Making

Too often, in all walks of life, people make "snap judgments"--sometimes regretable--when faced with problems which require decisions to be made and actions to be taken. Sometimes this process must be done quickly, e.g. military tactics responding to enemy movements on the battlefield, providing help to victims at the scene of an accident, etc. Other situations permit/require a more deliberate approach, e.g. starting a new small business, disciplining a problem employee or student, etc. Regardless of the time frame and circumstances, however, it is important to make the best decisions possible; and the ability to make timely, wise decisions is a skill much sought after in professional practitioners and leaders in all types of organizations. Figure (3) shows, in schematic format, the logical approach to problem solving and decision making in a business organizational scenario, while following a sequence of steps applicable to almost any situation, including scientific research. The process does not involve "rocket science", and should be quite easily understood and agreed to. However, a few of the steps are deserving of brief commentaries.

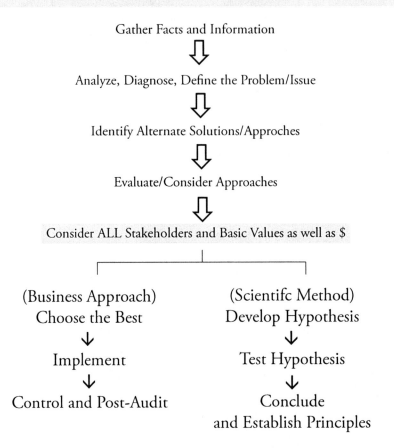

*Figure 3*

THE LOGIC OF DECISION MAKING, PROBLEM SOLVING, AND SCIENTIFIC RESEARCH

In attacking a problem, it is important to not focus primarily on the immediate situation without first searching for and analyzing the root cause(s) of the happening, condition, issue, opportunity, etc.. Then, means can be sought to attack or use underlying causes in concert with dealing with immediate symptoms of the problem. A simple illustration is to find ways to correct a student's belligerent attitude and poor grades. These symptoms could be caused by health problems, bullying by other students, family problems at home, deteriorating relationships with a girl friend/boy friend, etc., some of which might be subject to corrective action.

Of course, when immediate, short-term problems arise, it is well to be prepared by having done some contingency planning in advance, i.e. asking yourself "what should I do if different emergencies occur?". An excellent illustration of this may be seen in the January, 2009 occurrence wherein an experienced, well-trained airline pilot and flight crew made an emergency landing of a fully loaded commercial flight, saving the lives of all 157 passengers. This jet airplane left LaGuardia Airport and shortly therafter, during its ascent, hit a flock of birds--some of which were sucked into both of the airplane's jet engines, causing them to stall and be unable to restart. Without power, the airplane was destined to crash--perhaps in a highly populated area close to New York City.

Fortunately, drawing upon experience, training, wisdom, quick thinking, and skill, the pilot was able to glide the airplane to a water landing in the Hudson River; and the crew was successful in evacuating the airplane into the river from whence all of the passengers were rescued before the airplane sank. A truly heroic effort reflecting superb preparation, decision making, and skill.

This illustration highlights the Boy Scout motto, "Be prepared". As you progress through life, it is wise to periodically ask yourself, "what if .....?". Hopefully, as young parents of young children, you will not experience both being killed in a common disaster. However, if such would happen, who will take care of the kids? If, in a deteriorating economy as is being experienced in 2008, 2009, and on, I lose my job--how will I support my family and pay basic financial obligations?. Etc.

Here is a personal crisis situation which I experienced, reflecting a need for very fast decision making, but also a lack of adequate preparation. Shortly after graduation from Navy Officer Candidate School and subsequent training programs previously described, I joined my naval aviation squadron and found myself aboard an aircraft carrier assigned to a four month tour of duty in the Mediterranean Sea. One weekend, our ship anchored in the Bay of Naples and arrangements were made for large numbers of the ship's company to go ashore for "liberty" (touring, shopping, eating, drinking, etc.). I was assigned to be the officer in charge of one of the liberty launches used to ferry sailors from the ship to Naples and then back again. As a very inexperienced ensign, I was quite dependent on the coxswain, a third class petty officer, who ran the boat's engine and served as helmsman. However, I was the responsible officer in charge. Around midnight, we left the dock at Naples and embarked on the trip back to the ship with about twenty sailors on board, including a drunken wardroom steward named "Tiger Jones". This guy was an excellent middleweight boxer who won most of his bouts by knockout. About half way back to the ship, in the dark of night in the middle of the Bay of Naples, "Tiger" stood up in the launch and began to shadow box, challenging others to get up and spar with him--not a good and safe thing to do. Alternate solutions to this crisis problem were to: (1) grab him and push him down on his seat--not good to do dealing with an accomplished fighter; (2) threaten him with disciplinary action--likely to enrage "Tiger" in his inebriated state; (3) turn the launch around and go back to Naples--not wise since we were already half way back to the ship; and (4) order the other sailor/passengers to back away from "Tiger" and let him continue shadow boxing, but be ready to rescue him if he fell overboard. I chose alternate number 4 and, fortunately, after a few minutes of doing his thing, "Tiger" sat down and we made it back to the ship with no further incidents. I think I handled this problem as well as I could under the circumstances, but, if I had been better prepared with "what if" scenarios, I would not have allowed a rowdy, inebriated, potentially dangerous sailor to get into the launch without taking appropriate precautions; or insisted that "Tiger" and some friends stay in Naples until he sobered up.

In strategic planning, both corporate and personal, described earlier in this book, planners set objectives based on current situations and a most likely set of assumptions about the future. However, good planners will also consider a number of other possible scenarios which might come about and how to strategically deal with such changes, i.e. perhaps altering specific objectives and strategies.

Another illustration, more complex in nature, involves the need to learn and understand, in depth, the problem(s) of creating and maintaining unity and harmony in a church congregation. Politics are inescapable-- even in Christian organizations. Imagine the dilemma of a senior pastor of a large, established congregation, balancing the needs, feelings, and deep traditions of a wealthy establishment group, somewhat left-of-center theologically, which supports the church financially, vs. a group of newer, more energetic members who border on being evangelicals and want things the way they see them. Changing community demographics further compound the problem of declining membership. This particular pastor (mine) has succeeded beautifully in building and maintaining a spiritual, mission-oriented congregation (comprised of folks who genuinely like each other despite having some doctrinal differences) albeit being located in an urban setting which is some distance from where most of the members now live. He has done this by being a superb preacher, pastor, and community leader--meeting the needs of his flock for scriptural relevance and faith, while not offending people by hammering on doctrinal issues which have been interpreted differently by various denominational groups. Members of other Christian churches, as well as newcomers to our city, are voluntarily drawn to our church because of our pastor and who he is. The problem is: our pastor is now in his early sixties and chronologically approaching retirement in a few years. He will be extremely difficult to replace. What to do? Rules of the denomination prohibit promotion from within the congregation, i.e. associate pastor being elected to succeed a retiring senior pastor with whom he/she has been serving. I offer this as a realistic mini-case study, stating a problem in some detail and challenging you, the readers, to think about how you and your church would solve it--remembering to consider alternative solutions and not jump to conclusions.

The outline in figure (3) highlights consideration of all stakeholders and basic values--not just pursuit of profitabilty or some other tangible objective(s). For a business, stakeholders include not only stockholders (owners of the business) but also other groups of people impacted by the organization, i.e. customers/clients, suppliers, employees, and community--all of whom should be thought of in terms of fair dealings and well-being. The topic of Basic Values gets into the huge arena of ethics-- a subject far beyond the intended scope of this book. However, a good summary statement of ethical behavior to live by is embraced within the Golden Rule and the Four Way Test which members of the Rotary International service organization are expected to consider and follow in their dealings. This challenging set of ethical questions is:

> Is it the truth?
> Is it fair to all concerned?
> Will it build good will and better friendships?
> Will it be beneficial to all concerned?

Sometime in the late 1980s, I attended a series of lectures on ethics by Dr. Arthur Holmes, Professor of Philosophy at Wheaton College. Not being well schooled in philosophy, I had difficulty absorbing much of Dr. Holmes' shared wisdom. However, he presented an excellent summary of basic Christian thinking in development of Christian ethical behavior and management. This, I clearly understood, appreciated, and have remembered and used for many years. Dr. Holmes used an acrostic to teach his BPRC Approach to Christian ethics. The letter, B, stands for Base, which is God--from whom comes P, representing Principles,--upon which we base Rules,-- to be used in handling Cases involving ethics situations dealing with right and wrong and morality.

The two key principles, which are anchor points for the more specific considerations, are love and justice. This is worth remembering as you interact, particularly from positions of responsibility, with other people in all walks of life.

The recently popular rhetorical question, WWJD?, (What would Jesus do?) closely parallels in general the BPRC Approach.

The element of Control and Post-Audit simply means to observe and measure (where appropriate) progress actually being made and actual results attributable to the decisions which were made and the corresponding actions which were planned and undertaken--this in comparison with the original (or revised) objectives, strategies and plans. Unfavorable variances from what was planned generally call for corrective action to be taken, or revisions to be made in the plan.

## Some Good, General, Decision Making Tools

After progressing beyond the immature stage of wanting immediate gratification of desires, irrespective of costs and consequences, adults need to take a more cost conscious, value oriented approach to decision making. Perhaps the most familiar is to do a cost/value and/or a pros vs.cons analysis as a means of comparing alternate choices. Little needs to be said about about these relatively straightforward methods. In some situations, using a weighted factor comparison technique, as described in figure (1) will be very helpful. In this section, however, I want to present some less obvious, simple quantitative tools which should be useful to just about everybody. (You can learn about mathematical modeling and operations research in upper level college textbooks.)

Ratio Analysis is a means for making competitive value comparisons on a common basis, avoiding undue reliance on absolute numbers. This requires merely gathering and assembling appropriate data and then performing some simple division calculations, resulting in ratios of some number of units of something per some specific,selected base. As such, ratios provide a relatively pure means of comparison, often used as an important element in making choices. A few examples follow.

- Baseball players are evaluated and compared on the basis of many ratios, e.g. batting averages which are calculated by dividing total hits by total times at bat.
- Farmers may decide on how best to use their land (cattle vs. a variety of crops) on the basis of determining how to maximize profit (revenue received minus costs) per acre.
- Investors in the stock market are interested in many ratios, the most common of which might be the PE ratio, calculated by dividing the market price per share by the expected or recent earnings per share.
- Almost everyone must sometimes shop for food, and can be bewildered by displays of various products of various quality levels, in different packages containing varying quantities. How is a customer to intelligently decide on the best value which meets whatever quantity and quality level he/she desires. Here again, ratio analysis comes to the rescue by allowing comparisons in terms of price per unit of measure.
- Examples of the usefulness of ratio analysis are endless.

Benchmarking involves becoming a "copy cat", and why not? Organizations and individual people live in a competitive world where some type of ranking is quite normal. Certain scholars, doctors, teachers, athletes, factory workers, clerks, restaurant servers, etc. are very frequently picked out and known as "the best". The same is true of corporations, schools, churches, non-profit charities, small businesses, and governmental organizations. Benchmarking, in any competitive arena, calls for identifying top ranking entities,learning why they are considered superior, and then figuring out how to copy or do better in whatever factors cause the top ranking people or organizations to excel.

A "real life" example, using ratio analysis coupled with benchmarking, may be seen in the case of three large corporations competing in the production and sale of a certain chemical commodity, coming from single plant facilities dedicated to that commodity. Information available to the public enabled the COO (Chief Operating Officer) of Company "C" to see that the profit margin enjoyed by Company "A", in that commodity, was far superior to his company's. Exploring why this was so, he easily determined that the market prices at which this commodity was sold, by the three companies, was pretty much equivalent. Similarly, there could be little difference in the cost of the raw materials used in the product. Therefore, the problem had to reside in the cost of direct labor and overhead.

Exploring further, the controller exercised a legitimate form of industrial espionage. He arranged for observations to be made at Company A of the average number of railroad tank cars of the finished commodity leaving the plant each day and, similarly, the average number of cars parked in the employees' parking lot throughout each day. With this information, he calculated the approximate productivity ratio of gallons produced per employee hour worked, and found that Company A's productivity was significantly better than Company C's. He concluded that a reduction in Company C's workforce was needed, with no reduction in product output. A project was initiated to achieve this via attrition and employee transfers, and Company C's profit margin improved markedly.

Another device is the <u>Decision Tree</u> which, incorporating probabilities, helps managers to quantitatively view various actions which might be taken, starting from a given decision point, and what their likely effects will be. Figure (4) illustrates this technique using a very simple, yet realistic, case situation. Imagine a student, in his room at 9:00 PM, facing a tough exam early the next morning. He is tired and knows that he/she really should go to bed by midnight. How should he/she spend the next three hours?

Figure 4

## EXAMPLE: SIMPLE, REALISTIC DECISION TREE

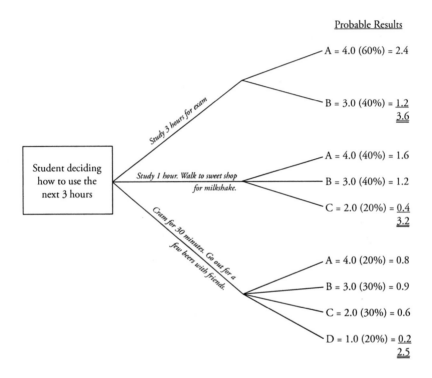

Probable Results

A = 4.0 (60%) = 2.4

B = 3.0 (40%) = 1.2
3.6

*Study 3 hours for exam*

Student deciding how to use the next 3 hours

*Study 1 hour. Walk to sweet shop for milkshake.*

A = 4.0 (40%) = 1.6

B = 3.0 (40%) = 1.2

C = 2.0 (20%) = 0.4
3.2

*Cram for 30 minutes. Go out for a few beers with friends.*

A = 4.0 (20%) = 0.8

B = 3.0 (30%) = 0.9

C = 2.0 (30%) = 0.6

D = 1.0 (20%) = 0.2
2.5

Conclusion: The student's test grade will probably drop from an A to either a B or C if he/she yields to either of the two temptations respectively.

Note that, in the diagram, the student is considering three alternate uses of his/her time--shown by the three "branches". The probable results stemming from each of the possible actions are calculated by identifying the possible grade points, associated with each result "branch", which might be earned, and then multiplying each possible grade point by the probabilty percentages of achieving such. In dealing with each alternate action "branch", the probability percantages used must add up to 100%. The sum of the multiplication products for each action "branch" then indicates the most likely grade he/she will receive if he/she chooses that "branch". In this case, the student would have to want an evening out, drinking with his/her buddies, pretty badly if it is going to cost him/her a probable drop of 3.6-2.5 = 1.1 grade points in the forthcoming exam.

This <u>Decision Tree</u> tool can be very helpful in a wide variety of situations, most of which are far more complex than the foregoing case. The key is to identify different, possible action "branches"; and then assign estimated, quantitative, possible results stemming from each action "branch"; and then multiply each result "branch" by a probability percentage, being sure that the percentages used for each action"branch" add up to 100%. Adding and comparing the multiplication products associated with each "branch" provides an quantitative indication of which of the alternative actions might be best, and what the comparative cost might be if other choices are made.

The <u>Nominal Group Technique</u> is another decision facilitating tool that is not well known--but very useful in situations where a group/committee must choose a "winner" from among a sizeable number of candidates (people, projects, etc.) without consuming a large amount of time. It is a thorough, fair, and democratic approach which results in a reasonable group consensus without wasting time in needless arguments. I first learned of this <u>NGT</u> while serving as an associate dean and department chairperson at Taylor University. A decision had been made to structure a month-long senior seminar course around a common theme to be used by all majors--with some time devoted to interaction between students majoring in different areas, and other time spent on theme-related issues specific to the individual majors. This was a good idea, but then it became the job of an assemblage of faculty department chairpersons to select the common theme. I faced our first meeting with feelings of fear and distaste, anticipating endless debate leading nowhere. As expected, about twenty different ideas were presented; but then the dean, presiding over the meeting, utilized the

Nominal Group Technique to reach a consensus/group decision in little more than two hours. Here's how we did it.

After a brief discussion about the overall objectives of the forthcoming senior seminar--to expand students' world views while enhancing their appreciation of the varied disciplines being taught at Taylor and the students involved therein--the competing senior seminar concepts were listed and their sponsors were invited to briefly present their respective reasons for such. A well-run general discussion followed, during which full participation by all attendees was encouraged. Then came a vote. Each committee member was asked to privately (on 5x7" cards) list his/her top five choices in ranked order of preference. These cards were summarized and the top five choices, chosen by the group, were identified. These five surviving concepts were then subjected to further discussion, looking for "pros and cons". This was followed by another vote, this time asking participants to select, from the five remaining candidates, their top three choices in ranked order. These second vote cards were then summarized and a winner was identified. The winning theme turned out to be a study of Israel and Greece, reflecting the history and present status of these two areas,and their impact on our Judeo/Christian heritage, science, business, athletics, literature, and the arts, etc.

Hopefully, you readers will remember the Nominal Group Technique,and the logical steps described in the foregoing paragraph, because it/they will be useful in many situations you are likely to encounter, e.g. selection of a scholarship winner from a group of worthy candidates, or a MVP (most valuable player), or a winner of a beauty pageant, etc.

Tied in with problem solving and decision making, it is very important that you--and all citizens in general--understand and appreciate the value of Basic Statistics, a subject which most college students love to hate. Almost every day, we are fed some sort of statistical information by the news media. What does it really mean? It is often said that " figures don't lie, but liars can figure". Without being totally false, some statistical presentations can be misleading; sometimes innocently and sometimes by design to support a position. You need to be prepared to challenge such data as you collect information for your personal enlightenment and use, or in pursuit of your employment responsibilities. For example, a recent article in our local newspaper said that 1/3 of our city's population live in poverty. However, what the article didn't say is that half of the number of citizens, with incomes less than the recognized poverty level, are college students who should not have been included in the aforementioned poverty ratio. Actually, fewer than 1/6 of our city's full-time resident citizens earn incomes lower than the poverty level.

Granted, advanced statistics can be somewhat "hairy" unless you are a good mathematician. However, there is no good reason for not knowing and using <u>basic statistical tools</u> such as measures of central tendency (mean, median, and mode), measures of dispersion (range and standard deviation), time series analysis, and seasonality--as well as the development and reading of charts and graphs. You will be a better informed citizen and employee if these tools are in your bag.

Finally in this section, I want to present the important concept of <u>Value Analysis</u> which was born during World War ll in an engineering and purchasing context. Far from being highly technical, however, <u>Value Analysis</u> has subsequently been accepted as a common sense approach, in all walks of life, to getting the most value (however that may be defined) from money spent to satisfy a need (either real or perceived).

During the early stages of the War, the enemy controlled large territories,and the Allies sometimes found it impossible to acquire some of the raw materials necessary to produce what was needed to fight and win. Therefore, substitutes for these materials were found and, in some cases performed better and cost less. After the War ended, an engineer at the General Electric Company, Lawrence D. Miles, reflected upon this usage of alternative materials, gathered data, and authored a book entitled Techniques of Value Analysis and Engineering. The book was/is particularly useful for design engineers and purchasing agents; however, the basic concept is quite simple, and applicable to just about everybody as they consider buying things and services.

My simple interpretation of Value Analysis is to first define the purpose/ function of what we are planning to design, make, or buy; and then find ways to satisfy that need/desire at the lowest cost. Key challenging questions to ask yourself, and then answer, about almost any item or service, are:

- What is it? What materials, skills, etc.are involved in producing it?
- What does it do? What function does it perform? What need(s) does it satisfy?
- What does it cost?
- What else will do the job?
- What would the substitute cost?

A few simple examples follow.

More than twenty years ago, if you stayed in a hotel or motel, you probably received two new cakes of soap. They were solid rectangular shapes, flat and smooth on both top and bottom. Their purpose was to allow guests to wash themselves at the sink and in the tub/shower. Each morning, regardless of whether a guest was checking out or not, a housekeeper would discard the used cakes of soap--even though they were only 20% used up--and replace them with new cakes. Let's say, for illustrative purposes, that the soap cakes cost the hotels/motels five cents each. Some smart person, using Value Analysis type thinking, reasoned that the purpose of this soap could be fulfilled, just as satisfactorily, with cakes containing significantly less material--and this resulted in soap cakes being reconfigured with waffle or concave surfaces while still maintaining the same outside dimensional envelope. This is what you encounter in motels today. Now, let's say that this slight change, in a seemingly insignificant item, saved two cents per day per room. In a motel/hotel enjoying an average occupancy of 100 rooms per night, this would amount to savings of $365 \times \$2 = \$730$ per year. A large chain of motels such as the Intercontinental Group (including the Holiday Inns), which operates well more than 2,000 hostelries, would gain more than $\$730 \times 2,000 = \$1,460,000$ per year from this simple application of <u>Value Analysis</u>. Beyond that, from a "green concern" standpoint, soap manufacturers are using less natural resources to provide products which get done what needs to get done. Also, a smaller volume of wasted, unused material gets dumped into compacted landfills.

Engineers and other designers have been increasingly concerned with <u>Value Engineering</u> in their creation of products. Complete textbooks and training seminars are devoted to this subject. At the most elementary level, consider fasteners which must hold things together with consideration given to strength, reliabilty, corrosion resistance, appearance, space utilization, etc.. In some situations where appearance is not a factor, why should a designer specify sets of stainless steel bolts, nuts, and washers to be used if all other factors can be met by identical hardware made from less costly cold rolled steel? Similarly, if a product,such as a sign,is needed to last no more than one year, why should it be painted with a top-quality, weather-resistant paint if a lower cost covering would provide a satisfactorily good appearance for that short a period of time?

Admittedly, the foregoing illustrations concentrated on functionality and were relatively easy to address. Yes, in everyday life, many other factors need to be considered, including personal pleasure (involving any of the senses--sight, touch, taste, smell, and hearing). Add to that features such as ego, social status, business/ organizational requirements, needs for exercise and relaxation, security, aesthetics, aging, overall comfort, family responsibilities, etc. For individual people, this requires folks to know themselves, their families, and their organizations, and truly understand what their values are and to what degree. If we wish to use Value Analysis to help decide between competing sources of products or services, we might calculate some value ratios for comparison purposes. This requires monetizing (real or estimated) of the different values being considered, and then plugging them into the following ratio equation.

Value ratio = (Functional use value + Other values, e.g. esteem)/ Cost

As a practical example, consider a situation in which you need to have a serious discussion over lunch with an important customer, client, or constituent. In the big city, you need to choose between three types of restaurants: (1) a nice sandwich shop across the street, where a decent lunch can be purchased for $10, but where the tables are crowded and the noise level is high; (2) a small, intimate French restaurant, also across the street, where a very good meal might cost $20, but where the tables are spread apart, the atmosphere is relatively quiet, and the head waiter takes you and your guest to "your table"; and (3) a classy restaurant in the city's most prestigious hotel, where a gourmet lunch might cost $50, in a nice quiet atmosphere, but where the head waiter treats anyone, not well known in the city's establishment, as a "nobody". Where should you take your guest? Check the following monetized values.

| Value Consideration | Sandwich Shop | French Restaurant | Prestigious Hotel |
|---|---|---|---|
| - Noontime nourishment (basic functional need) | 2 x $10 = $ 20 | 2 x $10 = $ 20 | 2 x $10 = $ 20 |
| - Meaningful discussion (for one full hour) | zero | $ 75 | $ 75 |
| - Esteem | zero | $ 20 | $ 5 |
| Total Estimated Value | $20 | $115 | $100 |
| Cost/Price | 2 x $10 = $20 | 2 x $ 20 = $ 40 | 2 x $ 50=$100 |
| Value Ratio | 20/20 = 1.0 | 115/40 = 2.9 | 100/100 = 1.0 |

Clearly, in this case, the French restaurant best meets your needs and provides the best value.

We could go on and on dealing with the subject of personal values, much of which is subjective and sometimes philosophical. That is not within the intended purview of this book. You will have many, many choices to make during your lifetime regarding the use of your resources to get what you need and/or just desire to varying degrees of intensity. I would only hope that you will find some of the tools, described in the foregoing sections, helpful in making sound decisions. A good question to ask yourself when working out your personal budget and sometimes considering questionable expenditures is, " Is this the best use of my money at this time and at this point of my life?"

# More Anecdotal Lessons
# About Alcoholic Beverages and
# Other Behavioral Matters

"Do you not know that your body is a temple of the Holy Spirit, who is in you, whom you have received from God? You are not your own:you were bought at a price. Therefore, honor God with your body" (1 Corinthians 6: 19-20 ... New International Version).

This biblical statement gives wise and strong admonition against anything, done purposely, which harms your God-given body; and this can be taken to mean, among other things, over-indulgence in alcoholic beverages and habit-forming drugs.

Yes, you can find references to wine in the Bible; and, yes, some recent scientific studies have indicated that an occasional glass of wine can be good for a person's heart; and, yes, my wife and I may occasionally enjoy a glass of wine with dinner. However, under no conditions are addiction and/or intoxication condoned. I have seen relationships, careers, and lives ruined by addiction to alcohol; and I have been closely aware of numerous incidents where party-induced drunkenness have led to fights, accidents, arrests, and even deaths. The biblical reminder that "your body is a temple of the Holy Spirit" and not to be mistreated should help you resist temptations regarding alcohol--and, most certainly, help you avoid experimentation with drugs which can be even more harmful, sometimes leading to crime and imprisonment. Of course, the potential bodily harm caused by tobacco usage--harm to both the user and folks subjected to second hand exposure--is well documented and will not be commented on further, other than to relate this to the aforementioned scriptural passage. So much for the brief sermon.

However, before I leave this substance abuse topic, I want to cite one more scriptural passage which I unknowingly violated once, and have felt badly about ever since. The Bible verse reads: "therefore,if what I eat (drink) causes my brother to fall into sin  (stumble), I will never eat meat again so that I will not cause him to fall" (1 Corinthians 8: 13 ... NIV). During three years of my career in manufacturing management, I served as production manager for a medium size company in the plastics industry. While there, I recruited and hired a young industrial engineer who immediately became useful and showed great potential.

A few months after his arrival, my wife and I invited this young bachelor to our home for dinner. Aileen, although of German descent, specialized in Italian cooking and prepared an excellent meal; consisting of antipasto salad, Italian bread, lasagna, tiramitsu (dessert), and Chianti wine. Glasses of the wine were poured and put at each place at the table. Jim drank the wine and ate heartily, and seemed to thoroughly enjoy himself. The next day, however, he did not show up for work and did not call in. He was absent again without notification the following day, and we began to worry about him. Tracking him down, we found him at an Alcoholics Anonymous facility where he had voluntarily turned himself in. Further investigation revealed that Jim was an alcoholic who had recently completed a treatment program at Alcoholics Anonymous and, after feeling obliged to imbibe at his boss' home,  felt emotionally disturbed to a degree that he felt it necessary to return to AA for more treatment. Can you imagine how  Aileen and I felt upon learning that we had caused this fine young man to stumble? There is a message here!

## Christian Tigers Need Frequent Feeding

The business world is tough, fast-moving, and very competitve. This is also true of many professions, non-profit arenas, and politics. It is very easy in this "rat race" world to ignore the presence of God in your life, and maybe even do some things you should not do. Daily devotions help to offset this worldly pressure, but, realistically speaking, left to our own devices and self discipline, this is often given low priority. For those guilty of this weakness (and for those not guilty) a weekly Bible study with friends and peers can be very beneficial. One of my favorite pastors, Tom Tewell, traveled from New Jersey to Manhattan every Wednesday to conduct a noontime Bible study for his parishoners and any others whom they might bring with them. Approximately forty executives brought brown bag lunches that day, and congregated in the board rooms of two major corporations which provided space.

Similarly, while teaching at Taylor University, I brought a number of Christian top level executives (mostly CEOs) of large NYSE companies to the campus to speak to students and local business owners and managers. Their topics frequently focused on business ethics, and many of them cited the importance of belonging to small accountability groups, comprised of folks having like stature, wherein they could share, in confidence, some of the ethics problems they face in their areas of responsibility.

Such small group study and sharing is very beneficial for Christian people at all societal levels and in all walks of life. Indeed, folks who affiliate with large Christian congregations, and find it difficult to fit in and become involved, will normally find friendships and help by joining a small group within the church --thereby making their overall church relationship all the more meaningful. In today's transient society, this is particularly true.

## Learn to Listen!!

Many of us, at times, have been guilty of "tuning out" people speaking in a meeting or in direct one-on-one conversations. Sometimes, we are bored; sometimes we have little respect for the speaker; and sometimes we are so filled with ourselves that we concentrate on what we are going to say next and essentially ignore what is being said to us. This is so very wrong--not only from a human relationship standpoint, but also from the liklihood that something truly of value will be missed. A great example of the benefits of listening, not only to superiors and peers, but also to folks who are employed and educated at lower levels follows.

In 1975, Governor Milton Shapp, of the State of Pennsylvania, authorized an exhaustive review of all administrative aspects of the executive branch of state government, looking for ways to operate more efficiently and effectively. Under the leadership of John Angle, recently retired from his position as Executive Vice President of U.S. Steel, and with advice from the consulting firm of Warren King and Associates, a team of 76 management-type people was assembled from Pennsylvania business organizations which voluntarily underwrote their participants' salaries and expenses. I was fortunate to be one of the six team leaders, reporting to John Angle, in this massive effort. The sixteen week review program was organized into six broad categories: Education; Welfare and Mental Health; Health, Hospitals and Correction; Human Resources; Financial Management; and Physical Resources.

The task force developed 412 recommendations, having a potential financial impact of approximately $505 million. Some of the recommendations came from bright ideas offered by task team members; but many resulted from conversations with state employees who had good knowledge about their areas of operation, had ideas for improvement, and were frustrated and eager to be heard. The task team captured these latent ideas and gave credit where credit was due. This is where real listening was/is involved. In all walks of life, at all levels of employment, good people have good ideas that deserve attention--even if they are not always doable. Failure to listen is tantamount to poor management, and leads to missed opportunities and lower morale among folks who want to be helpful but are ignored.

## Work Hard, Embrace Teamwork, but Look Out for Numero Uno

Giving a fair day's work for a fair day's pay has always been a good, minimal rule for all people to live by. In most organizations, compensation levels are structured on criteria such as knowledge, education, experience, responsibility, job conditions, and effort--and these payment programs assume that employers will get what they pay for. Of course, executive compensation at the highest levels defies the structural logic just described. CEOs and vice presidents of large organizations are often offered immense, seemingly obscene compensation packages to recognize their huge responsibilities, their competitive position in the marketplace, and the ego factor. I believe some adjustments are needed here.

From an employee's standpoint, truly earning one's pay should be a matter of honesty and integrity, such being included in the Judeo/Christian work ethic. "Goofing off" or otherwise failing to meet work expectancies will, at the very least, be detrimental to career growth. In many occupations today, these expectations can be based more on completing assigned projects or achieving specified levels of accomplishment than on "clock time" spent at the place of employment.

For those who want to progress upward on the career ladder, however, it is important to exceed basic expectations--in terms of cost, quality, or schedule; or all of the above. This means that motivated people should/must work hard and well--efficiently and effectively, doing things right and doing the right things--while still providing time and effort for family, church, community, and self-improvement. Normally, good work, equal to or above expectations, will be recognized and rewarded either monetarily or promotion, or both.

Working in a team context, in pursuit of common objectives, is usually much more pleasant than pursuing individual recognition in " dog-eat-dog" competition. Even in teams, however, individual performance can/should be recognized; but an important factor to be considered is a person's contribution as a team member. Much has been written and taught about the virtues of teamwork, such training often including participation in obstacle course programs which concentrate on recognizing and adapting to the strengths and weaknesses of the various participants, and also building trust.

The biblical parable of the talents, reported in Matthew 25, teaches the importance/obligation of people to use whatever God has invested in them (time, talents, and resources) actively and wisely. Similarly, the Apostle Paul exhorts Christian folks to "run in such a way that you may win" ... 1 Corinthians 9:24.

I, personally, have always worked very hard--sometimes to the detriment of family obligations and personal professional growth. Looking backward, I wish I had spent more time in scout leadership and coaching youth baseball and softball. (I was involved, but should have done more.). Professionally, I have two stories to tell, hopefully teaching lessons that you will appreciate.

At a fairly early part of my career, I worked as a contracts administrator in a small manufacturing plant acquired by a large corporation. In this role, I worked very hard and well, "keeping my nose to the grindstone" while secretly wishing I might be transferred to corporate headquarters in a marketing position. During this time, an even younger man was hired, also to work in contracts administration. He was bright and gregarious, and took time to "shmooze" with corporate executives when they visited the plant--during which time I continued to do what I perceived had to be done in meeting deadlines. Guess who got transferred to corporate headquarters. The lesson learned here is that building relationships, in a tasteful manner, is an important facet of organizational life, especially if such can be done without detracting from performance expectations which, in my situation, were self-imposed.

Subsequently, as I progressed in my career, I made sure to keep up with "cutting edge" developments in management/leadership theories and practices--by means of experience, graduate school education, professional organizations and literature, and attendance at professional conferences and tours. Indeed, early in the computer/information age, I was responsible for information processing at a manufacturing plant where the "mini" computer installation required a sizeable room to accommodate the equipment (key punching of cards, collating and sorting, processing, and printing).

However, after arriving at Taylor University, I allowed myself to become so overburdened with teaching, administration, projects, and community relations, that I allowed the accelerating progress of the information age to pass me by--resulting in my being only semi-literate in computer usage by the time I retired. To my embarrassment, some of my students were more adept in the use of computers than I was during my last few years at Taylor. I should have disciplined/forced myself to take advantage of training which was offered in computerized information processing rather than thinking that everything I was doing for Taylor was so indispensable that I couldn't afford to spend the time required for personal professional development and to stay current with the rapidly expanding information age. There is a lesson here. Again, look out for "numero uno" where such is within your updated plan for your career and life.

Do seek opportunities to attend meaningful professional conferences in your field(s) of interest. Good employers will provide time for you to do such, and will pay for your fees and expenses. Benefits include just getting away from the everyday routines and people; and also having a chance to "rub shoulders" with peers and experts in your field(s), listen to them, pick brains, and share ideas. Keynote speeches by ranking executives and smaller group seminars afford opportunities to keep abreast of developments; and also allow you to participate in discussions, give presentations, and become known--possibly causing new, attractive opportunities to open up for your consideration. Beyond the more formal meetings, walking around in the product display areas is an education in itself. Unencumbered by the details of your workplace, you can see what other organizations are doing. This can stimulate "free wheeling", creative thinking which may be beneficial when you return to your regular workplace.

Of course, conferences also allow you to expand networking contacts for the benefit of both your employer and yourself as you continue to look out for numero uno, even though you hopefully want to continue loyally working for your present organization. The benefits of networking are well known in career pursuits. In the "white collar world", more moves to new employers are probably brought about via network contacts than any other source

Networking is also valuable and important in many other walks of life. For example, upon leaving the Navy, I accepted a position with the Eastman Kodak Company, in Rochester, New York. I had never been anywhere near Rochester, and now I was to move my wife and two small children from our home area in suburban Philadelphia to upstate New York. Being Lutheran at that time, I decided to use this informal church network to find a reliable realtor in the Rochester area. Through a Lutheran pastor, I was hooked up with Walter Steffen who helped my wife and me find a home that was just right for us in Pittsford (a suburb of Rochester). Subsequently, Aileen and I became close friends with the Steffen family.

The foregoing illustration should not, however, be taken to encourage excluding folks of other races, religions, or ethnic backgrounds. Realistically, it is better to deal with highly capable, ethical practitioners--who are able to communicate with understanding--than to automatically shun such people in favor of less capable, less ambitious business and professional folks who happen to look and behave like you do. Of course, it is very comfortable if you can find top quality, honesty, integrity, and understanding in practitioners having beliefs and backgrounds similar to yours. That's where the "Christian Tiger" concept applies, i.e. business people and professionals who are competent and competitive, as well as caring and Christian.

Also, it is interesting and beneficial to take tours--most of them free--of various manufacturing and service operations where such are offered. It is a great learning experience to see how different products come into being and how other people work and make their living. I have enjoyed tours of automobile assembly plants, food processing, beer brewing, cigarette manufacturing, newspaper printing, stock markets, and a Federal Reserve Bank--such being available to citizens in general. Of course, in my roles as management consultant and professor of management, I was able to see many more operations, and learned much, even as I provided advice to clients and showed students what the real world is like.

### Protect the Dignity of Associates

A basic axiom is: "Praise in public. Reprimand in private". An associate's (subordinate, peer, or even superior) dignity is a precious thing. Demeaning a person in front of others is a very bad thing to do--bad for the person, and very likely bad for his/her future performance. Conversely, showing appreciation for a person will enhance self image, build loyalty, and lead to continued good performance, or even better.

Always give credit for good work performed by subordinates and peers. Never usurp credit. In fact, go out of your way to seek praise for others for their contributions. You will automatically, albeit quietly, be favorably recognized for your leadership. I remember one situation wherein a high level superior instructed a lower level associate to use company time to write a book on certain facets of management. The boss reviewed and approved the book and then had it published and took full credit for authorship. How wrong this was. Not only was it unfair and a violation of the principle of integrity, but this failure to give any credit to the real author became known and damaged the boss' reputation within his organization.

As you move up the responsibility ladder, disciplinary issues are bound to arise. Always try to handle them constructively at the lowest level possible. Remember that a key meaning of the word, "discipline", is training or to teach. Of course, there are different levels of wrongdoing, but most fall within a category that should first be dealt with by an oral reprimand and discussion. Repeated problems could then logically follow a chain of: written reprimand(s) placed in an employee's file, then some disciplinary action (like time off without pay), and finally termination. Successfully helping a subordinate associate get "turned around" is a rewarding experience, while firing an employee for cause is a very sad event.

Interestingly, the Bible offers a somewhat parallel approach to discipline. In Matthew 19, dealing with conflict situations, Jesus is quoted as telling his followers to first go to a "brother" who offends you. If that doesn't resolve things, take some witnesses with you and meet again with this "brother". Failing in this effort, the next step is to take the issue to the church as a whole; and, if things still can't be worked out, go to the civil authorities. I have personally observed, in church congregations where persons should have known better, two situations where teaching elders, who felt themselves aggrieved, ignored the biblical steps and went directly to ruling bodies higher in the church administration which, in turn, handled both cases poorly. This caused considerable stress and some needless loss of membership in the involved congregations.

It is wise, nice, and motivational for leaders and managers to share "big picture" issues with all associates. The story is often told of the stone mason who enjoyed his work because he knew he was helping to construct a magnificent cathedral vis-a-vis the mason who saw his job as merely laying stones to earn a living. Knowing why they are asked to do certain things, in concert with an overall effort, will usually cause employees to be happier, work harder, and sometimes even contribute valuable suggestions. Furthermore, if employees know that their superiors are genuinely interested in them, and want to help them succeed, they will form a healthier, happier, more productive work force.

In the early 1900s, Frederick W. Taylor became known as "the father of scientific management", using work measurement to create time standards which became the foundation for individuals being payed on a piece work incentive basis. Dr. Taylor was most concerned about production output, and cared little for workers' feelings and dignity. I believe that productivity, top notch quality, and meeting schedules should be rewarded, but preferably in a team context or profit sharing mode. Public posting of individual performance records--or, student grades in a school scenario--can be embarrassing, demeaning, and demoralizing.

Yes, individual efforts must be watched and recognized--in the workplace, schools, and other endeavors--and those who can't, or won't, "hack it" must be dealt with, but such should be handled privately. Nor should there be a policy, known to be the case in some companies, to annually identify a group of employees, ranked at the bottom, and replace them. Similarly, in education, I do not believe in grading on a curve, where the number of As is limited and some students are destined to get Ds or Fs. Good managers and teachers will set high expectations; but will also attract, develop, and motivate workers and students such that they all can be rewarded with incentive recognition or As or Bs if they meet or exceed the established goals.

## Some Thoughts About Gambling

The Bible offers no clear instructions regarding gambling. (Yes, the account of Jesus' crucifixion tells of Roman soldiers casting lots to determine who would get which items of his garments--but this is hardly encouragement for anyone to get into gambling.) The Bible is, however, very clear about exercising good stewardship with whatever you have. In this context, one must wonder if God would be pleased with our use of time and money playing various games of chance or wagering in other ways. I am sure He would be very displeased if we risk more than we can afford to lose.

Consider the unskilled worker who has difficulty supporting his family, but nonetheless spends five to ten dollars per week on state lotteries, hoping to "strike it rich" but perhaps denying his family things that they need while so doing. At the other extreme, think about the affluent individual who considers it "fun" to lose $100 to $1,000 or more in a night of poker, or at the casino. (Recognize that casino organizations--both government sponsored and private enterprises-- take a significant cut out of lottery revenues, reducing the value of potential winnings well below what the "pot" would be if only chance is involved.)

Gambling can be addictive. Just once in my life, I played the slot machines in Reno, Nevada--starting with nickels and building up to quarters--and I found it hard to stop. I won just enough, combined with losing, to keep me going. Surely, I was going to hit it big on the next pull ?? Fortunately, I had only $25 to start with (this was pretty big back in the 1970s), and when it was gone, I had to quit. I learned a valuable lesson. However, I have seen some very prominent people ruin their careers as a result of gambling addiction. I have also watched young professionals get lured into poker games with high level superiors at company parties, starting with playing for a nickel a chip, but then, under subtle pressure, escalating to a quarter a chip. Some of these "kids" lost as much as $200 and had to go home and explain this to their spouses.

Repeating: If you must gamble--for whatever reason--never risk more than you can afford to lose; and, recognizing that you are likely to lose, ask yourself, "is this the best use of my money right now?" How much better it would be if that money were donated to a worthy charity.

## Don't Be Afraid to Ask for Favors or Suggest Improvements

As a member of an organization, it is always wise to communicate through the established "chain of command" in both directions--up or down. Failure to do so may easily damage morale and upset people being bypassed. This advice is pretty obvious. However, outside your organization, if you have a truly attractive, well-thought-out request or idea, it is a good strategy to contact decision-making executives as high up as you can reach with practicality--and such people can be total strangers. A written proposal, letter, or memorandum is usually the best way to start; and this means you should be able to write well--clearly, briefly, accurately, and using good structure, vocabulary, and grammar. Many high level executives have administrative assistants and staff employees who screen incoming correspondence, and send only important, interesting items on to the "boss" for awareness and/or action. However, a top quality submission of a good idea or meaningful request will usually get through, and may lead to a friendly, appreciative, and helpful response. Do not be afraid to ask at high levels!

In the early 1960s, I was a low-mid level manager working toward a Masters Degree in Business Administration (MBA). It was a time when the American public was very much concerned about poor business ethics being practiced by a number of large corporations. A classic case involved some companies engaged in the processing of asbestos and fabrication of products made therefrom. Management, including company doctors, learned of the toxic nature of asbestos but did nothing about it, nor did they disclose this to their employees--many of whom developed lung cancer (often fatal). This, and similar situations, prompted me to write my masters' thesis on the subject, " Can Business Managerial Ethics Be Codified?". I developed a reasonably straightforward questionnaire and mailed it, accompanied by an explanatory letter, to the Chief Executive Officers of the top 100 firms listed in the New York Stock Exchange. Surprisingly, I got a 60% response, mostly from the CEOs themselves. Obviously, they were interested in the topic and wanted to see the results of my study. This illustrates how top level people will often respond helpfully if properly approached.

Most of the responding executives expressed interest, but were skeptical about the practicality of developing and enforcing codes of ethics dealing with issues as complex as those faced in the business world. For my report, I had to write about my "null hypothesis", but I did receive a good grade. Interestingly, however, today most sizeable business organizations do have meaningful codes of ethics which are promulgated to all their stakeholders (employees, stockholders, vendors, customers, and community), and hopefully followed in their organization's behavior.

Similarly, while teaching at Taylor University, I enjoyed great success asking many top level executives, e.g. Bowie Kuhn, Commissioner of Major League Baseball, to visit the Taylor Campus and talk with students, faculty, administrators, and local business leaders about the role of Christian ethics in various walks of life. This was a topic in which they had experience and knowledge, and a desire to share with receptive audiences.

One more example, again at Taylor University. As we developed our new, experiential learning course called "Free Enterprise Laboratory", our plan was to create three student-run business organizations in the fields of retailing, manufacturing, and consulting. Eighteen junior and senior level students were to be enrolled each semester, and divided into three management teams of six students each. Working with real money, each team's assignment was to develop and present a business plan, gain approval to be funded, launch and run their business throughout the semester, and shut then it down (hopefully showing a small profit), completing their project with a professional-quality comprehensive report. For this, each student would earn four credits and a grade. Space to conduct these three businesses was obtained from the school, but we needed a substantial amount of seed money to provide working capital with which the businesses could be started. I presented a comprehensive proposal to the Chairman and CEO of a sizeable, privately held corporation and he responded with encouragement and a donation in the mid five digits. The course prospered and was very popular with students who were fortunate enough to get in. Upon graduation, they found this experiential learning to be very advantageous in their job searching. Also, the course gained nationwide recognition and an award from the Freedoms Foundation. Again, the point of this story is: (1) conceive something that is attractive, appealing and useful; (2) prepare a proposal and presentation thoroughly and professionally; and (3) don't be afraid to ask for help.

## America is Still a Land of Opportunity--<u>But</u> You Must Use Common Sense, Study and Work Hard, and <u>Provide Something of Value</u>

It is vitally important that you manage your personal finances wisely. Our American society, and the whole world in general, is currently experiencing the worst economic depression since that of the early 1930s. There is no need to dwell on this other than to say that we, as a people, have largely brought this on ourselves as a result of our growing materialism, felt need for immediate gratification, and a willingness to gamble resources in very risky investments.

William Shakespeare, in his famous tragedy, "Hamlet", gave birth to a well-known quotation which is rather appropriate today. In the play,

Lord Polonius advised his wayward, problem son, Laertes, "Neither a borrower nor a lender be: For loan oft loses both itself and friend, and borrowing dulls the edge of husbandry". I, personally, have made four significant loans to family members and friends, only one of which has been fully paid back. Beyond that, Shakespeare's word, "husbandry", can be taken to mean wise stewardship and management of resources. Admittedly, this admonition by Polonius is not totally applicable today, but it should give rise to more thoughtful financial management than has been prevalent in recent years.

Yes, our capitalist free enterprise system does require credit in order to operate and grow as successfully as we have; but, when corporations, banks, and other financial organizations unconscionably promote needless products, e.g. derivatives, which provide no tangible value, are very risky, and primarily enrich just a few top level manipulators of money; and when the public eagerly accepts opportunities to spend more than they can afford to obtain immediate possession of luxuries and "get rich quick" schemes; we courted disaster and got what we deserved.

You, individually, cannot solve our societal problems, but you can use your resources and talents wisely as God would expect you to do. Here are a few tips.

- Establish a personal budget, balancing expected incomes and expenditures, and stick to it.
- Use credit cards for your convenience and advantage only-- not the profitability of banks and other issuing institutions. Pay off balances every month, avoiding the very high interest rates charged on unpaid amounts.
- Remember the Lord in your budget with a definite amount or percentage of income.
- When the time comes to purchase a house, limit your housing expenditures (mortgage payments, real estate taxes, and home owner's insurance) to approximately 31% of gross income.

- Save/invest something every pay period--for "rainy day" needs, kids' college costs, retirement, etc.
- Never, except in the most dire emergency situations, patronize a cash-in-advance-of-a-paycheck provider. Interest rates charged are outrageous !

Here are a few examples of folks I have met who have started at relatively low positions, taken advantage of the opportunities offered in America, and achieved a high degree of success.

- Don Seibert (recently deceased) began his career with JCPenney as a shoe salesman in a small store in Bradford, Pennsylvania. Twenty seven years later, he became Chairman of the Board and Chief Executive Officer of this huge retailing company. As he achieved success at ever increasing levels of responsibility, Don never wavered from his sense of Christian ethics and personal values, and became an inspirational leader within the Penney organization, his communities (business and civic), and his church. His story and advice have been published in a book, The Ethical Executive, published by Simon and Schuster, Inc. in 1984.

- Marta Gabre-Tsadick was born in poverty in Ethiopia, but rose to become the first female senator in the government of Emperor Hailie Selassie. However, in 1974, military powers overthrew Emperor Selassie and it was necessary for Marta to flee, along with her husband, Deme, and three sons. After a hazardous escape to Kenya and then a move to Greece, again living in poverty conditions, the family received a church sponsorship which allowed them to come to the United States where they estblished residency in Ft. Wayne, Indiana. Here, Marta and Deme searched for a way to earn money to live and provide an education for their children. A possible opportunity was found in a government publication which listed products and services to be purchased by the Federal Government. One particular product was a sizeable quantity of small parachutes for sonobouys, allowing these sensitive, submarine-sensing devices to be dropped from naval airplanes and land gently in the water. Deme wrote a proposal and was awarded a significant contract to make these parachutes. Deme and Marta proceded to rent a small building, purchase a few industrial sewing machines and other equipment, recruit and hire a small workforce (mostly immigrants), and successfully completed the contract--thereby starting a job-shop type business which has built a good reputation, enjoyed growth, and is still active today. As they prospered, Marta and Deme established a charitable organization called " Project Mercy " which endeavors to provide food, clothing, health care, and education for impoverished people who continue to live in their Ethiopia homeland. Marta was also elected to serve on the Board of Trustees of Taylor University wherein she shares her global experience, Christian insight and wisdom. Here is an inspirational example of courageous people working very hard and taking advantage of the opportunities available in America.

- A few years ago, my wife and I took two grandchildren to Chicago, and, while there, went to Wrigley Field to see the Cubs play. Traveling by taxi cab, I was seated in the front passenger seat beside the driver who was a native of India, legally living and working in America with a visa arrangement. I noticed that this young man had a college textbook on corporate finance sitting on the console beside him. Responding to my questions, he told me that he was nearing completion of an associates degree in business administration, and that he was working sixty hours per week, sharing a relatively cheap apartment with four other Indians, and saving as much money as he possibly could. His goal was to save $250,000 with which he would then return to India, marry, start a business, and live very happily. I had to admire his determined pursuit of a challenging, admirable objective; and his willingness to live very frugally as he strove to achieve it as quickly as possible.

- One last example: In retirement, I sometimes do grocery shopping for my wife. I have learned to appreciate and admire the associates (managers, clerks, cashiers, stockers, and baggers) at a nearby store which is part of a sizeable, regional chain named Marsh Hometown Market. These associates work very efficiently and effectively; yet take enough time to recognize regular customers, share a few pleasantries, and be helpful. Most of them know the locations of just about everything in the store, and are able and willing to serve in a variety of functions, e.g. cashiers doing bagging, stocking, serving at the customers' utility bill paying counter, etc.. Many of them have been employed at this store a long time. Turnover is very low. When asked why, the response is generally that they are treated well by management, they love <u>their</u> customers, they consider this store to be <u>their</u> store, and they like and take pride in what they do. The staff of this store makes it very pleasant to shop there, and I am willing to pay a reasonable premium for the enjoyment of dealing with these competent and pleasant people. These folks are not destined to become CEOs, board members, or financiers--<u>but</u>, they too are successful and happy.

How then should we define "success"? Wealth, power, fame, prestige ...? Not necessarily ! Some extremely rich, powerful people have been known to lead very lonely, unhappy lives. Success formulae vary widely among different individuals. Consider the major success ingredients to which different people give varying weights: serving others, family, career, church, community, country, profession, avocation, etc.. A Christian summer camp in central Pennsylvania teaches campers to think in terms of their motto, "I'm third--(1) God, (2) family, (3) me". I, personally, as I matured, became increasingly influenced by the opening words of a famous hymn, "Take my life and let it be, consecrated Lord to thee ...". I truly believe that real success is an individual thing, beginning with each person knowing himself/herself and then using his/her God-given talents and interests as well as possible in whatever environments he/she finds herself/himself--giving appropriate weightings to the factors listed above. Jesus' parable of the talents, told in Matthew 25, provides a good set of principles to live by, i.e. work hard and well, and avoid slothfulness.

Christian thinking and behavior is very much needed, at all levels, in all walks of life throughout the world today. Success is to be found in providing this. **Doing well in whatever you do earns the right to be heard and exercise influence.** Sometimes, this involves selfless service, and sometimes it requires intense, albeit fair, competition to attain high ranking, powerful positions. I believe it to be very important for people, adhering to Christian teachings, to be present in the ruling structures of government, business, education, healthcare, entertainment, law, church, etc.--and that they exercise their voices and power, in a reasonable manner, to strive for what is right. Just imagine what our country and world might be like if dominated by atheists and/or radical proponents of other religions. For the sake of future generations worldwide we must not let this happen. Therefore, we Christians must compete with skill, energy, imagination, ethics, and excited vision for a better world. Thomas L. Friedman's two recent books, The World is Flat and Hot, Flat and Crowded, do an excellent job of documenting what is happening to us and what we must do to reverse the dangerous trends.

# A Few Business Axioms--Applicable Also to Churches, Schools, and Other Non-Profit Organizations

### Start-Up Considerations

Many people dream of starting and running a small business in which he/she is the owner and boss. Many try it and fail, often as a result of not doing their "homework" before committing significant amounts of time and money to endeavors which never really had a chance to succeed. This is particularly true of folks who see themselves as good cooks and therefore think they should be successful in the restaurant business. Without adequate analysis and planning, many of these well-intentioned entrepreneurial efforts go "belly up" in a short time. This is not meant to discourage you from acting on your dreams, but rather to set forth a few basic considerations which, if followed, will help to promote success and avoid failure.

Begin by identifying a consumer need, or strong desire, which you can satisfy with a superior, excellent product or service--giving close attention to your potential market (the quantities of each product/ service which you can sell, at various price levels, in different geographic/ demographic areas). A few examples follow:

- A suburban community in eastern Pennsylvania was inhabited by relatively affluent to upper-middle-class families. Many chain grocery stores were available, but the quality of their produce (fruits and vegetables) ranged from bland to sub-par. There were mild complaints, but nothing was done to correct this. A smart resident recognized this as an opportunity and opened a small specialty store called "Center Fruit" wherein he offered discriminating customers a selection of top quality produce which he personally procured from food distribution centers in Philadelphia. The shop became popular and prospered, and the proprietor expanded his offerings to include fancy cheeses, top quality lunch meat, crackers and bread. Then came other gourmet lines, and soon "Center Fruit" became a destination which customers would go out of their way to patronize.

- I spent much of my life in Pennsylvania and New Jersey where it was easy to find local bakery stores which featured home-made pastries. Such neat small businesses are rare in central Indiana where I now live. However, in Muncie, a city of about 65,000 people, a man named Concannon recognized this "vacuum" as an opportunity and developed a superb bakery, offering a wide variety of pastries and breads, and expanding into gourmet popcorn and top quality chocolate candies. Customers from a large geographic area regularly come to Concannon's Bakery to purchase his products and/or visit his recently opened second store which also features a sit-down restaurant which offers soup, sandwiches, salads, pastries, and beverages (including a gourmet coffee bar).

Concannon's has become a very significant asset in the economy of Muncie and Delaware County, including employment of many residents as well as appropriately rewarding this outstanding entrepreneuer.

- Another example involves a more technical type person in central Pennsylvania who recognized that many thermoplastic materials (organic materials which can be melted and shaped over and over again), such as nylon, acrylic. polycarbonate, and tetrafluoroethylene

(Teflon) could be shaped via processes such as casting, molding, and extrusion; and used for many more applications than was then the case, e.g. combs and womens' hose. After some experimentation, he arranged to purchase quantities of nylon combs which he then melted down and used to produce tubing and other mill shapes which had beneficial physical properties which justified customers paying premium prices for such. He expanded this concept into other thermoplastic materials, and, from this humble beginning, a company evolved enjoying sales well over $20,000,000 per year.

Niche positions are ideal, i.e. product/service lines which are not so large in scope that they will attract difficult competition. For example, a company continues to thrive making mechanical fuel pumps for automobiles and other applications involving internal combustion engines--this despite the fact that almost all automobiles, currently manufactured, use fuel injection systems rather than mechanical fuel pumps to feed their engines. There is still a limited,ongoing market for the mechanical pumps for older cars and other special applications. This company stands almost by itself as the supplier of this product line--a comfortable position.

Similarly, an inventor-type man needed a small, profitable business to financially support his development of a very significant new composite material. He recognized a need, throughout Northern America, for custom sized O Rings. An O Ring is a circular sealing device, with a round cross section, used to prevent liquids from flowing into unwanted locations having circular cross sections. Materials used for the O Rings vary according to specific liquids to be sealed, heat conditions, etc.. Standard O Rings can be easily purchased at hardware stores and other supply houses. However, when a standard O Ring will not do the job, a special, non-standard O Ring must be found somewhere. My inventor friend filled this need by employing two ladies who, using very primative equipment, could extrude the required type of material, in the required cross sectional shape and to the required circumferential length, and then bond the extruded and cured material to meet the circular requirement. Thus were custom O Rings made, for which high prices were paid. This was a very lucrative small business which enjoyed a very special niche.

Find ways to gain and maintain a competitive advantage. Keep aware of the market for your products and/or services--also, who your competitors (current and showing interest in entering the field) are and what they are doing. Above all, practice the Japanese principle known as "Kaizen" which means continuous improvement--in cost, quality, and service. Teach your associates to continually challenge what they see and do, rhetorically asking themselves, "Isn't there a better way to do this?--Are lower cost materials available which will do the job just as well?--Can we improve the appearance and/or functionality of our product?--etc."

Whole textbooks have been written on the subject of Small Business Management and should be accessed by persons considering such a venture. Indeed, most of the material presented in these books is also applicable to non-profit organizations, schools and churches. I have no desire to produce a condensed version of this good information in this book, but I do want to enthusiastically endorse your making use of Small Business Development Centers (SBDCs) whose mission it is to assist in the "formation, growth, and sustainability of small businesses and to develop strong entrepreneurial communities". One area in which they are particularly strong is that of helping budding entrepreneuers prepare a sound business plan which is needed to acquire financial aid; and, even more important, cause the would-be business person to better understand what he/she is getting into. To illustrate this point, I have listed the topics needed to be covered in a good business plan, such being taken directly from the table of contents of a publication entitled <u>Your Business Plan</u>, prepared by the Small Business Development Center of Indiana and made available for folks who seek counseling.

- Summary
- Your Mission Statement
- Goals and Objectives
- Background
- Management
- Use of Technology
- Description of Products/Services
- Price/Quality Relationship
- Competitive Advantage
- Location
- Marketing Strategy
- Promoting the Business On-Line
- Sales Forecast
- Cash Flow Projections
- Projected Income Statement
- Break Even Analysis
- Balance Sheet
- Debt
- Fixed Assets
- Salaries and Wages
- Start-Up Expenses
- Timetable
- Supporting Exhibits

Assuming you have successfully completed and presented your business plan, gained the necesary financial support, and gotten your business up and running, you would be wise to revisit your business plan at least every year, making revisions as appropriate.

## Understanding the Relationship of Incoming Revenue, Fixed and Variable Costs, and Profit or Loss

In most cases, engaging the services of a professional accountant and attorney is a wise thing to do. However, a college degree in accounting is not necessary to understand and use the "Break Even Analysis" which I will describe, in simple terms, in this section. Failure to do so has resulted in the failure of many small businesses, non-profit endeavors, and charitable fund raising events--that probably should never have been started--with considerable investment of time, emotion, and money. First, a few definitions:

- Incoming revenue is a direct function of the quantity/volume of goods and/or services sold, expressed generally in dollars. It is the product of unit price times the number of units sold.
- Fixed costs are those which must be paid irrespective of the volume of goods sold. Examples are: rent, utilities, insurance, interest on loan(s), etc.
- Variable costs are those which increase in a direct relationship with the volume of goods sold. Examples are: materials and labor directly related to the production of products or the provision of services.
- Price is the dollar amount charged to sell a unit of product or service.
- Margin is the difference between price per unit and variable cost per unit. It is the dollar amount per unit which is used to help offset the aggregate of fixed costs and hopefully provide a profit.
- Profit is the amount remaining after paying all variable costs and fixed costs.
- Break even is the volume of goods or services sold at which total incoming revenue exactly equals the total of variable costs plus fixed costs, yielding no profit nor loss.

The following simple equations express the basic, important truths of "Break Even Analysis".

The volume at which a firm will just break even, with no profit nor loss

$$\text{Price x } \underline{\text{Volume}} = \text{Fixed Cost} + (\text{Variable Cost per Unit x } \underline{\text{Volume}})$$

or

$$\underline{\text{Break Even Volume}} = \text{Fixed Costs/Margin}$$

If a certain profit is desired, the volume needed to attain such is shown below

$$\underline{\text{Desired Volume}} = (\text{Fixed Cost} + \text{Desired Profit})/ \text{Margin}$$

Admittedly, fixed costs will grow by steps as an organization grows, and variable costs may drop with increased productivity, but the foregoing relationships remain valid at all levels. The basic message, which is so often ignored, is that a certain amount of fixed costs will attend all business-type ventures and must be paid off regardless of how little product or service is sold. We are seeing an example of this, at a macro level in 2008 and 2009, as automobile manufacturing companies struggle with the problem of selling too few cars to offset the fixed costs of excess capacity, servicing large debts, and paying contractual health care and retirement benefits to a very large number of retirees.

This important relationship applies not only to businesses of all sizes, but also to schools which are funded by tuition payments, church congregations which are financed by members offerings, and one-time fund-raising events such as fairs and concerts sponsored by counties or communities

Figure (5) is an illustrative chart showing the type of <u>Break Even Analysis</u> which should be considered by an entrepreneur who would like to start up a small restaurant.

Let's say that the following fixed costs have been identified:

| | |
|---|---|
| Rent | $1,000/month |
| Insurance | 200 |
| Electricity | 100 |
| Telephone | 50 |
| Heat & Air Conditioning | 100 |
| Water & Sewage | 50 |
| Interest on Loan | 200 |
| Cook's Wages | 2,400 |
| Helper's Wages | 1,600 |
| Two Servers' Wages | 750 |
| Advertising | 200 |
| Maintenance | 300 |
| Charitable Gifts | 50 |
| Miscellaneous | <u>200</u> |
| Total Fixed Costs | $7,200 |

Let's also say that variable costs for food and supplies are estimated at 40% of the price of each meal.

Therefore, the restaurant's margin will be 60% of incoming revenue, and :

Break Even Volume, in dollars, will be:  Fixed Cost/Margin = $7,200/0.6 = $12,000 per month.

If that sales volume is unlikely, the entrepreneuer would do well to find another source of income.

Most small business textbooks will expand on this truth in greater detail. However, no matter how much you tweak the definitions of fixed and variable costs, the fact remains that some fixed costs will exist and must be paid, using margin which can be varied by increasing prices and/or volume and/or reducing variable costs.

*Figure 5*

# ILLUSTRATIVE BREAK EVEN ANALYSIS CHART

(Startup of a Small Restaurant)
(Estimated Revenues & Costs on Monthly Basis)

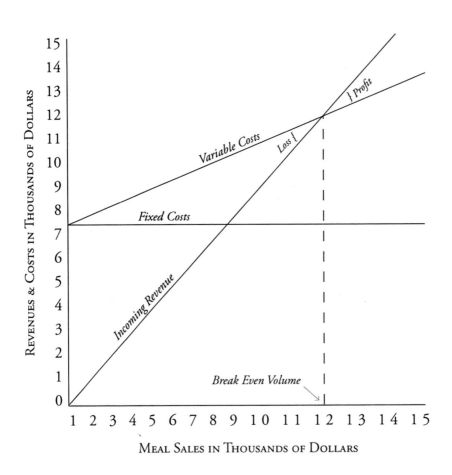

# Thoughts on Management and Leadership

## General

Many, many complete books have been written on these subjects, authored by renowned experts--both academic and successful practitioners. Some of my favorites include: Peter Drucker, Tom Peters, Stephen Covey, Ken Blanchard, Jim Collins, Warren Bennis, Michael Porter, Rosabeth Moss Kanter, John Gardner, and John Maxwell. Regardless of your current position or aspirations--whether to become a CEO, operations manager, school principal, entrepreneur, church pastor, politician, team captain, scout leader, etc.--it behooves you to read some of the excellent literature in the fields of management and leadership, and learn to apply many of the key principles--particularly those which blend well with the unique person you are.

## Management

First, a classic definition, attributable to Lawrence Appley during the time he was president of the American Management Association: "Management is the art and science of getting things done through the use of people and other resources". Please note that I have underlined the words, "getting things done". Management connotes responsibility for achievement, and it involves both a "soft side" (art) and a "hard side" (science). Dealing with people requires tact, understanding, sensitivity, good communication skills, and an ability to be firm and inspirational. At the same time, managers must be able to apply proven methodologies which may often be quantitative and/or technical. Managerial positions abound in all facets of society and in a large range of levels, e.g. branch manager of a bank, shift manager at a fast food restaurant, athletic director at a college, supervisor of a manufacturing department, regional sales manager, etc. It is a very satisfying role to be able to organize a team and achieve important goals.

Almost all management textbooks identify four main functions of management, applicable to any field of endeavor. These are: planning, organizing (including staffing), leading, and controlling (comparing actual accomplishment with planned objectives, and taking corrective action if necessary). Each of these functions merits a number of chapters in a management textbook, and I have no intention of addressing these topics in any depth. However, I do want to discuss the two general types of leadership, i.e. transactional vis-a-vis transformational.

Within the overall context of managerial leadership, the focus is primarily on getting the job done--achieving objectives and goals set by top level leaders. This is transactional leadership--the type of leading practiced by most managers at most levels.

In 1982, Tom Peters and Bob Waterman wrote a book entitled, <u>In Search of Excellence--Lessons from America's Best- Run Companies</u>. I want to share with you some of the words used by the authors to describe excellent managers, hoping that you will commit them to memory as I have done. In a general sense, an excellent manager is: a <u>pathfinder, a decision maker, and an implementer</u>. In leading people, an excellent manager is: a <u>coach, cheerleader, facilitator, and nurturer of champions</u>. Think about these descriptors. The first group implies being empowered by higher authorities to find new or improved methods and having the "guts" to implement them. The second group is more people oriented and encourages managers to work hard at helping their associates succeed in their lives and careers. I, personally, have found great satisfaction in performing my managerial roles as described above. Two quotations from famous people are suitable here.

- " The growth and development of people is the highest calling of leadership" ... Harvey S. Firestone

- " A major function of leadership is to produce more leaders, not more followers" ... Ralph Nader

## Transformational Leadership

Most readers of this book will become transactional leaders, in one form or another, during their lifetimes. A much smaller number will have the ability, motivation, and opportunity to become transformational leaders. Such people are usually to be found in the top level positions of organizations, ranging in scope from national to local and involving a wide variety of endeavors. Within this category, only a small percentage perform as truly transformational leaders. This type of leadership almost always involves conceiving visions of improvement--challenging but attainable--and then communicating such to team members in ways that excite and motivate, resulting in success and fulfillment. Transformational leaders look at "big picture" issues, relative to their areas of responsibility, and allow themselves to dream about major, important improvements which could be achieved with imagination and hard work by committed followers. Of course, such dreams can achieve or approach reality only if they are shared with teams of highly motivated leaders who, in turn, will skillfully lead others in excitedly pursuing the goals and objectives related to the dream(s).

Some examples of well-known transformational leaders are: Dr. Martin Luther King (famous for his " I have a dream" speech and subsequent leadership in efforts to reduce racial discrimination);

President Franklin D. Roosevelt (for his efforts to improve the American economy after the severe depression of the early 1930s); and Prime Minister Winston Churchill (for his heroic leadership of the British nation from the threshold of defeat to victory in World War ll). Hopefully, our current President, Barack Obama, will earn a similar, highly-respected place in history. The need and opportunity is certainly there.

On a smaller scale, think of Bill Gates and Steve Jobs and their contributions to the emerging information era; Tony Dungy and his development of the Indianapolis Colts into Super Bowl champions (based on teamwork, vision, hard work, and decency); Lee Iacocca leading the Chrysler Corporation from the verge of bankruptcy to profitablity in the 1980s; Bill Hybels developing, from nothing, the tremendously influential Willowcreek megachurch; Millard Fuller and his creation of the Habitat for Humanity organization which builds and provides decent, low cost housing for needy but ambitious families; etc.

On a still smaller scale (within reach of many of you), think of local political leaders who rebuild run-down communities; coaches who develop championship programs embracing skill, motivation, and character building; pastors and church leaders who aim for their congregation to grow significantly in all forms of ministry; schools and hospitals striving to be recognized as "the best" in their fields; etc.

I, personally, changed careers and came to Taylor University with a vision of helping create the best business, accounting, and economics program within the Christian College Coalition. Fortunately, my colleagues embraced the vision, and we enjoyed success.

Please note the need for vision in transformational leadership that will make a difference for good. My family and my church use the more modern translations of the Bible, but I thoroughly embrace the King James Version interpretation of Proverbs 29:18 which says," Without vision, the people perish". People, in all walks of life, will perform better and be happier if they know why they are doing something and believe in it. It is up to transformational leaders to provide such visions. Another appropriate quotation came from President John F. Kennedy: "The problems of this world cannot be solved by cynics whose horizons are limited by obvious realities. We need those who can dream of things that never were."

## Confidence and Humility

This is an important, albeit sometimes difficult to achieve, blend for both transformational and transactional leaders. In 2001, Dr. Jim Collins, formerly of Stanford University, authored a best selling book (still on the best selling list in 2009) entitled <u>Good to Great</u>. For this outstanding publication, Collins and his research team used some very difficult criteria to identify eleven top ranking, "good" companies which had become truly "great" companies and maintained that superb rating for fifteen or more years. Surprisingly, the top leaders of these great organizations were/are, in Jim Collins' words,"self-effacing, quiet, reserved, even shy--a paradoxical blend of personal humility and professional will".

This finding provides a stark contrast with the image often associated with top level tycoons such as the managing partner of a financial hedge fund whose story was reported in the March 31, 2009 issue of <u>The Wall Street Journal</u>. This person reportedly told a friend that his real job was "to live better than any of his clients", and that he did. His lifestyle included an apartment in Manhattan, mansions in London and Madrid, a chauffeured car and private jet, a Falcon yacht, and a hacienda on the Spanish island of Mallorca. He hosted lavish parties, collected expensive works of art, and entertained royalty and glamorous females. He would do well to read and follow John Bogle's book, <u>Enough</u>. Bogle truly earned his position of wealth and respect by founding and leading the Vanguard family of mutual funds, but shunned lavish living such as described above.

This leads to a few closing comments. Some years ago, it was faddish to promote the concept of servant leadership by showing an inverted triangle, with the broad base at the top and the pinnacle at the bottom. This was meant to show that customers and the lowest level of employees are really the most important, and that successive layers of supervision and leadership are less and less important, and that the top leader is least important of all. There is some truth in this if we view increasingly higher levels of management and leadership being provided greater and greater opportunities to serve humanity-- particularly if the leaders are primarily motivated to serve others instead of self enrichment. However, to ignore the traditional organizational structure,which is normally depicted by an upright triangle with the top executive at the peak and the work force at the bottom, is nothing less than faddish nonsense. If organizations are to achieve objectives and goals, there must be structured levels of responsibility and authority. Yes, enlightened management has moved away from the old "bull-of-the-woods" style of supervision where the "boss" demands that things be done just because he/she says so--to a much more effective and efficient use of teams wherein folks, having a variety of skills and characteristics, work together toward common objectives, in an environment of trust and mutual respect. Indeed, servant leadership, within logical organizational structures, is a valid and very desirable concept but only in the context stated above and exemplified in the motto of the Rotary Club, "Service above self".

Finally, let me say that competition is not a bad thing. Indeed, it is a very good thing. Played fairly and truthfully within the boundaries of laws, decency, and Christian ethics, --and with compassion for disadvantaged people--competition leads to continual improvement as we have experienced in America. This is vastly different from the stagnation we have seen in countries which have embraced communism.

In international and domestic dealings, it continues to be important to gain and maintain a competitive advantage. It is not good to negotiate from a position of weakness if such can be avoided. Think how much better the world will be if America continues to be powerful and respected, and pursues issues with a sense of Judeo/Christian ethics, than if the balance of power shifts significantly in favor of radical elements which shun freedom and embrace violence as a means of getting their way. Please, gratefully embrace your country, America, and the Judeo/Christian faith and principles available to you, and do your very best to serve with the God-given talents you have been blessed with.

**Become a Christian Tiger (competent, competitive, caring, and Christian) if you are not already one, and earn the gravestone epitaph at the end of life, "well done, good and faithful servant".**

# A few classic quotations worthy of remembrance:

"All that is necessary for the triumph of evil in the world is that enough good people do nothing."...
　　　　Edmund Burke, British statesman and philosopher, 1729-97

"And what does the Lord require of you but to do justice, love kindness, and walk humbly with your God." ... Micah 6:8

"I expect to pass through this life but once. If there is any kindness, or any good thing I can do to my fellow beings, let me do it now. I shall pass this way but once." ... W.C. Gannett

"God grant me the serenity to accept the things I cannot change; courage to change the things I can; and wisdom to know the difference." ... Reinhold Niebuhr

"From everyone who has been given much, much will be demanded; and from the one who has been entrusted with much, much more will be asked." ... Luke 12:48 (NIV)

Lightning Source Inc.
LaVergne, TN USA
14 August 2009
154798LV00003BA/16/P